Hittite Prayers

**Writings from the Ancient World
Society of Biblical Literature**

Simon B. Parker, General Editor

Associate Editors

Jerrold S. Cooper
Richard Jasnow
Anne D. Kilmer
Ronald J. Leprohon
Theodore J. Lewis
Peter Machinist
Gregory McMahon
C. L. Seow

Volume 11
Hittite Prayers
by Itamar Singer
Edited by Harry A. Hoffner, Jr.

Hittite Prayers

by
Itamar Singer

Edited by
Harry A. Hoffner, Jr.

Society of Biblical Literature
Atlanta, Georgia

HITTITE PRAYERS
Copyright © 2002
Society of Biblical Literature

No part of this work may be reproduced or transmitted in any form or by any means, electronic or mechanical, including photocopying and recording, or by means of any information storage or retrieval system, except as may be expressly permitted by the 1976 Copyright Act or in writing from the publisher. Requests for permission should be addressed in writing to the Rights and Permissions Office, Society of Biblical Literature, 825 Houston Mill Road, Atlanta, GA 30329 USA.

Library of Congress Cataloging-in-publication Data

Singer, Itamar.
    Hittite prayers / Itamar Singer ; edited by Harry A. Hoffner, Jr.
      p. cm. — (Writings from the ancient world ; no. 11)
    Includes bibliographical references and indexes.
    ISBN 1-58983-032-6 (pbk. : alk. paper)
    1. Hittites—Prayer-books and devotions—English.
    I. Hoffner, Harry A. II. Title. III. Series.
BL2370.H5 S54 2002b
299'.199—dc21
                                            2002004720

Printed in the United States of America
on acid-free paper

Contents

Series Editor's Foreword	ix
Abbreviations	xi
Explanation of Signs	xiii
Acknowledgments	xv
INTRODUCTION	1
THE TEXTS	19
I. EARLY INVOCATIONS	21
1. Invocation of the Sun-goddess of the Netherworld against Slander (CTH 371)	21
2. Invocation of the Sun-god and the Storm-god against Slander (CTH 389.2)	24
3. Invocation of the Sun-goddess of Arinna for the Protection of the Royal Couple (CTH 385.10)	25
II. EARLY EMPIRE PRAYERS	29
4. Prayers to the Sun-god for Appeasing an Angry God (CTH 372–374)	30
4a. Prayer of Kantuzzili (CTH 373)	31
4b. Prayer of a King (CTH 374)	33
4c. Prayer of a Mortal (CTH 372)	36
5. Prayer of Arnuwanda and Asmunikal to the Sun-goddess of Arinna about the Ravages of the Kaska (CTH 375)	40

	6. Hurrian Prayer of Taduhepa to Tessub for the Well-being of Tasmi-sarri (CTH 777.8)	43
	7. Prayer to the Sun-goddess of Arinna Concerning Plague and Enemies (CTH 376.C)	44
III.	MURSILI'S PRAYERS CONCERNING PLAGUE AND ENEMIES	47
	8. Mursili's Hymn and Prayer to the Sun-goddess of Arinna (CTH 376.A)	49
	9. Mursili's Hymn and Prayer to Telipinu (CTH 377)	54
	10. Mursili's "Third" Plague Prayer to the Sun-goddess of Arinna (CTH 378.III)	56
	11. Mursili's "Second" Plague Prayer to the Storm-god of Hatti (CTH 378.II)	57
	12. Mursili's "First" Plague Prayer to the Assembly of Gods and Goddesses (CTH 378.I)	61
	13. Mursili's "Fourth" Plague Prayer to the Assembly of Gods (arranged by localities) (CTH 378.IV)	64
	14. Mursili's "Fifth" Plague Prayer to the Assembly of Gods (arranged typologically) (CTH 379)	66
IV.	MURSILI'S PRAYERS CONCERNING HIS WIFE AND HIS STEPMOTHER	70
	15. Mursili's Prayer to Lelwani for the Recovery of Gassuliyawiya (CTH 380)	71
	16. Mursili's Prayer to the Sun-goddess of Arinna for the Recovery of Gassuliyawiya (CTH 376.F)	73
	17. Mursili's Accusations Against Tawannanna (CTH 70)	73
	18. Mursili's Exculpation for the Deposition of Tawannanna (CTH 71)	77
V.	MUWATALLI'S PRAYERS	80
	19. Muwatalli's Prayer to the Storm-god Concerning the Cult of Kummanni (CTH 382)	81
	20. Muwatalli's Model Prayer to the Assembly of Gods through the Storm-god of Lightning (CTH 381)	85
VI.	PRAYERS OF HATTUSILI, PUDUHEPA, AND TUDHALIYA	96
	21. Hattusili's Prayer of Exculpation to the Sun-goddess of Arinna (CTH 383)	97

22. Puduhepa's Prayer to the Sun-goddess
    of Arinna and Her Circle for the
    Well-being of Hattusili (CTH 384) 101
23. Fragments of Prayers to the Storm-god
    of Nerik (CTH 386.1-3) 105
24. Tudhaliya's Prayer to the Sun-goddess of Arinna
    for Military Success (CTH 385.9) 108

Sources 111

Concordance 117

Bibliography 119

Indexes 133

Series Editor's Foreword

Writings from the Ancient World is designed to provide up-to-date, readable English translations of writings recovered from the ancient Near East.

The series is intended to serve the interests of general readers, students, and educators who wish to explore the ancient Near Eastern roots of Western civilization, or compare these earliest written expressions of human thought and activity with writings from other parts of the world. It should also be useful to scholars in the humanities or social sciences who need clear, reliable translations of ancient Near Eastern materials for comparative purposes. Specialists in particular areas of the ancient Near East who need access to texts in the scripts and languages of other areas will also find these translations helpful. Given the wide range of materials translated in the series, different volumes will appeal to different interests. But these translations make available to all readers of English the world's earliest traditions as well as valuable sources of information on daily life, history, religion, etc. in the preclassical world.

The translators of the various volumes in this series are specialists in the particular languages and have based their work on the original sources and the most recent research. In their translations they attempt to convey as much as possible of the original texts in a fluent, current English. In the introductions, notes, glossaries, maps, and chronological tables, they aim to provide the essential information for an appreciation of these ancient documents.

Covering the period from the invention of writing (by 3000 B.C.E.) down to the conquests of Alexander the Great (ca. 330 B.C.E.). the ancient Near East comprised northeast Africa and southwest Asia. The cultures represented within these limits include especially Egyptian, Sumerian, Babylonian, Assyrian, Hittite, Ugaritic, Aramean, Phoenician, and Israelite. It is hoped that Writings from the Ancient World will eventually produce translations of most of the many different genres attested in these cultures: letters—official and private—myths, diplomatic documents, hymns, law collections, monumental inscriptions, tales, and administrative records, to mention but a few.

The preparation of this volume was supported in part by a generous grant from the Division of Research Programs of the National Endowment for the Humanities. Significant funding has also been made available by the Society of Biblical Literature. In addition, those involved in preparing this volume have received financial and clerical assistance from their respective institutions. Were it not for these expressions of confidence in our work, the arduous tasks of preparation, translation, editing, and publication could not have been accomplished or even undertaken. It is the hope of all who have worked on these texts or supported this work that Writings from the Ancient World will open up new horizons and deepen the humanity of all who read these volumes.

Simon B. Parker
Boston University School of Theology

Abbreviations

ABoT	*Ankara Arkeoloji Müzesinde bulunan Boğazköy Tabletleri*
AoF	*Altorientalische Forschungen*
BiOr	*Bibliotheca Orientalis*
Bo	Inventory numbers of Boğazköy tablets excavated 1906-1912
Bo year/...	Inventory numbers of Boğazköy tablets excavated 1968ff.
CANE	*Civilizations of the Ancient Near East* (Sasson 1995)
CHD	*The Hittite Dictionary of the Oriental Institute of the University of Chicago*
ChS	*Corpus der hurritischen Sprachdenkmäler*
CoS I	*Context of Scripture I* (Hallo 1997)
CTH	*Catalogue des textes hittites* (Laroche 1971)
FHG	*Fragments hittites de Genève* (Laroche 1951-52)
FHL	*Fragments hittites du Louvre* (Durand/Laroche 1982)
HbOr	*Handbuch der Orientalistik*
HED	*Hittite Etymological Dictionary* (Puhvel 1984-)
HEG	*Hethitisches Etymologisches Glossar* (Tischler 1977-)
HFAC	*Hittite Fragments in American Collections* (Beckman/Hoffner 1985)
HW	*Hethitisches Wörterbuch* (Friedrich 1952).
JAOS	*Journal of the American Oriental Society*
JCS	*Journal of Cuneiform Studies*
JNES	*Journal of Near Eastern Studies*
KBo	*Keilschrifttexte aus Boghazköi*
KUB	*Keilschrifturkunden aus Boghazköi*
MARI	*Mari Annales de Recherches Interdisciplinaires*

OLZ	Orientalistische Literaturzeitung
Or	Orientalia
RHA	Revue Hittite et Asianique
SMEA	Studi Micenei ed Egeo-Anatolici
StBoT	Studien zu den Boğazköy-Texten
StMed	Studia Mediterranea
THeth	Texte der Hethiter
TUAT	Texte aus der Umwelt des Alten Testaments
VBoT	Verstreute Boghazköi-Texte
ZA	Zeitschrift für Assyriologie
.../a-.../z	Inventory numbers of Boğazköy tablets excavated 1931-1967

Explanation of Signs

Single brackets [ ] enclose restorations.
Angle brackets < > enclose words omitted by the original scribe.
Parentheses ( ) enclose additions in the English translation.
A row of dots . . . indicates gaps in the text or untranslatable words.

Acknowledgments

First and foremost I would like to thank Professor Harry A. Hoffner, Jr., who initiated the preparation of this volume, carefully read through the manuscript, and made many valuable suggestions. I also wish to thank the series editor, Professor Simon B. Parker, whose remarks helped me in refining my English formulations. Thanks are also due to Professor Heinrich Otten, who generously allowed me to utilize the fragment 1193/u (join to Hattusili's Prayer, no. 21). I have often profited from conversations, oral and written, with Volkert Haas, Jörg Klinger, Craig Melchert, and Frank Starke, as well as with my former students Yoram Cohen, Amir Gilan, and Jared Miller. I thank all these friends and colleagues for their suggestions and insights, but I assume final responsibility for any remaining inadequacies or inconsistencies.

I dedicate this book to my wife Graciela.

Tel-Aviv, January 2002

Introduction

When the gods hear my word, they will put right the bad thing which is in my soul and remove it from me.

Muwatalli II

The Corpus

Prayers were among the first Hittite texts to be transliterated and studied in the earliest days of Hittitology (see, e.g., the refs. cited in Güterbock 1958: 237, n. 1, and in Singer 1996: 1). The first efforts toward more complete philological editions of groups of prayers were A. Goetze's study of Mursili's plague prayers (1930), and O. R. Gurney's dissertation on Mursili's prayers (1940), both of which have stood the test of time admirably. Translations of well-preserved Hittite prayers were later included in various compendia on ancient Near Eastern literature, in English (Goetze 1950; Kühne 1978; Beckman 1997a), German (Kühne 1975; Ünal 1991), French (Christmann-Franck 1989), Dutch (de Roos 1983), and Spanish (Bernabé 1987). E. Laroche's seminal paper on the vocabulary and typology of Hittite prayers (1964) was followed by many articles which provided overviews of the genre within the context of Hittite religion and literature (e.g., Houwink ten Cate 1969; Kammenhuber 1974; Güterbock 1978; de Roos 1995). Prayers other than Mursili's were edited (Friedrich 1957; von Schuler 1965: 152ff.; Houwink ten Cate/Josephson 1967; Haas 1970: 175ff.), and several articles dealt with the structure and literary history of Hittite hymns and prayers and their indebtedness to Mesopotamian prototypes (Güterbock 1958; 1964;

1974; 1980; Reiner /Güterbock 1967; Marazzi/Nowicki 1978; Marazzi 1981; Carruba 1983). G. Wilhelm provided a first glimpse into the yet poorly understood group of Hurrian prayers and hymns, which are of utmost importance for the study of cultural contacts between Mesopotamia and Anatolia (1991; 1994). The only anthology of Hittite prayers was published by R. Lebrun in 1980, the transliterations and translations of which are in need of revision (see the reviews by Kellerman 1983 and Marazzi 1983). Several new editions of individual prayers have appeared since (Sürenhagen 1981; Tischler 1981; Hoffner 1983; Archi 1988; Singer 1996; de Martino 1998). A full philological re-edition of the entire corpus of prayers, including unpublished fragments from Boğazköy and elsewhere, is an urgent desideratum, as are further comparative studies with other ancient Near Eastern corpora. A serious comparison of Hittite and biblical prayers (see, provisionally, Greenberg 1994) can only be accomplished by the inclusion of the *tertium comparationis,* i.e., the Babylonian prayers, which exerted a considerable influence on all other Near Eastern cultures (Wilhelm 1991: 39).

One of the difficult tasks in devising a volume dedicated to Hittite prayers is defining the parameters of this genre with regard to neighboring ones, such as hymns, conjuration rituals, oracular inquiries, etc. The Hittites (as most traditional cultures for that matter) followed a "holistic" approach in their dealings with the divine world in a difficult situation.[1] They investigated its causes through oracular inquiries, invoked the gods by various evocation rituals, pleaded their case in prayers, conciliated the offended god(s) through hymns of praise and expiatory sacrifices, and vowed them presents. All these and other actions formed part of one integral procedure attempting to regain the gods' good will and support. Many a Hittite eyebrow would probably have been raised in view of our endeavor to systematically classify and divide the various religious texts into well-defined categories. From their point of view, a more sensible and effective procedure would be a comprehensive consideration of *all* the actions needed to counteract a certain problem until a harmonious situation is restored. Such general investigations surely exist, but more often the various categories of religious literature are studied separately, and this volume forms no exception. Thus, a brief explanation of the criteria for excluding certain categories from this collection of Hittite prayers is due.

Hymns and prayers are usually considered together in compendia dedicated to ancient Near Eastern religions.[2] The distinction between the two is not clear-cut, depending mainly on the relative proportion of the praise directed toward the god and the suppliant's plea in a given text. Most prayers contain at least some short praise for the addressed god, and even a hymn dedicated entirely to the adulation of a certain god alludes, at least indirectly, to the devotee's hope for divine guidance and general well-being.[3] In some of Mursili's prayers (nos. 8–9) the hymnic introduction takes up about a third of the text, whereas in the so-called Plague Prayers (nos. 10–14) it is almost entirely missing. However, the decision to exclude proper hymns from this volume was not dictated by the length of the hymnic part in a given prayer, but by an entirely different consideration. Except for the Babylonian hymn to Shamash, which was adapted and incorporated into Hittite prayers to solar deities (nos. 4, 7, 8), all the foreign hymns (to the Sun-god, the Storm-god, and Ishtar) discovered at Boğazköy seem to have had strictly educational functions, such as scribal training and scholarly interest, and did not serve any "practical" cultic purposes (Wilhelm 1994: 70). This applies not only to Sumerian-Akkadian hymns (CTH 793–795), but also to hymns which have been furnished with a Hittite translation (CTH 312, 314, 792.1), and even to a hymn which is preserved only in a Hittite version (CTH 313), but whose Babylonian origins are evident (Güterbock 1978: 128; Wilhelm, ibid.). These literary texts should be studied and presented in juxtaposition with their Mesopotamian prototypes (as, e.g., in Reiner/Güterbock 1967), perhaps in a volume which would also include other types of translated Mesopotamian literature, such as lexical texts, omina, and legends (e.g., Gilgamesh). For similar reasons I have also excluded the long bilingual Hurrian-Hittite hymn to Ishtar (CTH 717; see Archi 1977; Wegner 1981; Güterbock 1984; Wilhelm 1994: 70ff.), the exact origins of which remain to be established.

Oracular inquiries aimed at discovering the reasons for divine wrath can often resemble prayers for exculpation from the discovered sins. Hattusili declares himself innocent in several suspected offenses against various persons (no. 21), and similar lists of political errors are contained in two fragmentary texts generally dated to Urhi-Tessub/Mursili III (CTH 297.7 and CTH 387; see Houwink ten Cate 1994: 240ff., with bibliography; see also van den Hout 1998: 46ff.; Parker 1998: 282ff.). CTH 297.7 could be a prayer directed to the Sun-goddess of Arinna and the Storm-god of Hatti (Houwink ten Cate 1974: 135), but other classifications are also possible, e.g., a trial procedure (as classified in CTH) or a *mantalli* ritual (for which see CHD L–N: 176bff., with literature; van den Hout 1998: 5f.). At any rate, the text is too fragmentary for a connected translation.

Rituals of offering ceremonies are as a rule appended to every prayer, but only rarely is the ritual part recorded or preserved (see *Ritual Context*); and conversely, almost every ritual contains some short invocation or praise to the god. But except for large prayer portions embedded in a ritual text (as in the substitution ritual and prayer for Gassuliyawiya, no. 15), the extensive genre of Hittite rituals and oracle texts has not been mined to extract short prayerlike passages (see, e.g., Collins 1997: 164f. for CTH 716).

Besides these thematic considerations, the state of preservation also played a role in the choice of texts included in this volume. There are dozens of small prayer fragments which still await identification and joining to larger texts (CTH 385–386, 389). Only if considerable portions of a prayer are preserved, or can be safely restored, is it worth inclusion in a volume of translations. An exception has been made, however, in the case of no. 6, in order to call attention to a group of prayers written in Hurrian.

After this sifting process there are still two dozen prayers or large prayer fragments in the volume, which justifies considering the Hittite prayer as a literary genre of its own (*contra* Kühne 1978: 165). Contrary to the general orientation in Hittitological studies, which are mostly concerned with a structural analysis and a diachronic investigation of the literary history (*Überlieferungsgeschichte*) of a given prayer or groups of prayers, I have ventured a more synchronic or subject-oriented approach. The texts are grouped in several thematic-chronological clusters, each dealing with a certain problem, such as the plague, or the sickness of Gassuliyawiya. I thought it more expedient to provide for the general reader interested in Hittite religion an overview of the situations which prompted prayers, rather than to follow the highly intricate literary tradition of a text and its prototypes.[4] Still, the basic information on the state of preservation of each text, its duplicates and parallels, and its putative literary history, is briefly indicated in the introductory sections, together with bibliographical references. For similar reasons of convenience I have provided full translations of each individual text, even if large parts of it are duplicated by parallel versions (as in the case of nos. 4a–c). This provides not only a continuous reading of a textual unit in its entirety, but also the possibility of juxtaposing and comparing the versions. As for the countless gaps and breaks typical of most Hittite tablets, I have provided restorations only if supported by parallel passages or sound logic. Tentative restorations are indicated by question marks, whereas more problematic ones are discussed in footnotes. I have tried to refrain, however, from exceedingly daring and unwarranted restorations, which risk perpetuation in general studies.

Function and Terminology: The Prayer as the Enactment of a Case in a Divine Court

Since the earliest days of Hittitology, the most common designation for "prayer" has been recognized in the verbal noun *arkuwar,* derived from the verb *arkuwai-* (Hrozný 1919: 153). Subsequent studies, especially Laroche's study on the vocabulary of Hittite prayers (1964: 13ff.), have pointed out that *arkuwar* (cf. Latin *arguo, argumentum*) is a juridical term, referring to the presentation of a plea, an argumentation, or a defense against an accusation (cf. further Houwink ten Cate 1969: 82ff.; Lebrun 1980: 426ff.; Sürenhagen 1981: 136ff.; Singer 1996: 47ff.; Melchert 1998: 45–47). The same word is used when a servant justifies himself before his master, when a vassal king argues his case before his suzerain, or when two Great Kings take their dispute before the Divine Court. The structure and rationale of a Hittite prayer is best understood as the enacting of a case in a divine court. This accords with the typically Hittite way of approaching all relations between two parties in legalistic terms. The defendant is the king, the prosecutor is the offended god, the advocate is the addressed deity (requested to act as an intercessor), and the court of justice is the assembly of gods. The prayer is presented by the king or his representative with all the features of a lawsuit, including the confession of or exculpation from guilt, the presentation of mitigating circumstances, and the inveigling of the divine judges with flattery (hymns) and presents (vows). What is obviously missing is the "final verdict" disclosing whether the defendant's arguments have been accepted, and whether his requests for health, long life, prosperity, victory over enemies, and divine support in general would be granted. Unlike other Near Eastern cultures, the Hittites apparently did not compose prayers of thanksgiving. They expressed their gratitude to their gods through pious deeds, such as the erection and embellishment of temples, or the dedication of cult objects, sometimes inscribed with dedicatory texts.[5]

The various terms that are often considered to represent different types of prayers (Lebrun 1980: 414ff.), are in fact parts of the overall composition. From Mursili II onwards, the *arkuwar,* i.e., the pleading, constitutes the main part of the text. In earlier prayers the emphasis is more often laid on the *mugawar* (or *mugessar*), "invocation, entreaty" (of the deity's presence through an evocation and offering ritual), derived from the verb *mugai-,* "to invoke, to entreat". Partly synonymous verbs are *talliya-,* "to evoke," and *sara huittiya-,* "to draw out, attract". Sometimes the *mugawar* ritual is inscribed on a separate tablet (see colophon of no.

8). The verb *walliya-* describes the praising of the god, but there seems to be no specific designation for the hymnic opening of a prayer (Güterbock 1978: 132). Finally, the verb *wek-* is used to express the suppliant's "wish, request, petition" of his divine judges. A typical Hittite prayer contains, in different proportions, all these elements, but rarely are all of them preserved (as in no. 20).

The preserved preambles and colophons refer variously to the "invocation" of a certain god (as in no. 8), or, more often, to the "pleading" addressed to him (nos. 9, 11, 12, 19). For unknown reasons, a colophon is missing altogether from some prayers (nos. 21–22). The few preserved incipits of Hittite prayers refer to the crisis which induced the composition. The plague prayers of Mursili are spoken "when [the people] of Hatti [. . .] are dying . . ." (colophon of no. 8.E; cf. no. 11). The model prayer of Muwatalli is spoken "if some problem burdens a man('s conscience)" (no. 20, §1). Another typical occasion for royal prayers (not specifically mentioned in colophons) was an imminent and important military campaign. For example, at the beginning of Mursili's reign he invoked the Sun-goddess of Arinna with the following short prayer, quoted in his annals: "Sun-goddess of Arinna, my lady, side with me and defeat for me those hostile neighbors who regularly disparaged and humiliated me and forever were bent on taking possession of your territories, O Sun-goddess of Arinna, my lady" (de Roos 1995: 1997).

"The Defendant": The King or His Representatives

Most, if not all, recorded Hittite prayers are spoken in the name of the king, either by himself, or by an official (scribe and/or priest) praying on his behalf (see below). Most exceptions can easily be explained. The influential queen Puduhepa prays for the recuperation of her ailing husband (no. 22), and probably a similar situation generated the Hurrian prayer of Taduhepa (no. 6). The earliest prayers (nos. 1–2) are not sufficiently preserved to disclose their authorship, but they clearly deal with the defamation of the king. The only unusual case is posed by the parallel prayers for appeasing an angry god, nos. 4a–c. In no. 4b the speaker is an unnamed king; in no. 4a the speaker, Kantuzzili, is a prince and high priest speaking on behalf of his king (see below, *Evolution of Hittite Prayer*); no. 4c is put in the mouth of a "mortal," which I doubt refers to a simple commoner.[6] Rather, it is intended to emphasize the suppliant's mortality and fragility, also expressed in pessimistic reflection upon the human condition in the prayer itself: "Life is bound up with death and death is bound up with life. A human does not live forever. The days of his life are counted. Even if a human lived for ever, and evil sickness of man were to be present, would it not be a grievance for him?" (no. 4c, § 11 = no. 4b, § 5').

In the last analysis, the corpus of Hittite prayers is restricted to kings, or, in rare cases, to other members of the royal family. Prayers of the ordinary pious, as in Babylonia or Egypt, have not been found in Hatti. To be sure, the king prays not only for his and his family's health and success, but even more so for his land and his people. Mursili's ultimate argument for divine mercy is the perishing of Hatti's population in the plague, rather than his own safety.

The king often refers to himself in the prayers as "the priest," because, as head of the cultic hierarchy, he bears the title "Priest of the Sun-goddess of Arinna" (Houwink ten Cate 1987). If not otherwise stated, the praying ceremony was performed by the king himself.[7] The exceptions found in several of Mursili's prayers only prove the rule. In the prayer to the god Telipinu it is explicitly stated that "the scribe shall read out daily this tablet to the god," and then the scribe himself is quoted saying: "Mursili . . . and the queen . . . sent me, saying: 'Go, invoke Telipinu, . . .'" (no. 9, §§ 1–2; cf. no. 8, § 1 and no. 11, § 1). On the other hand, in prayers which state "I, Mursili . . . am pleading/bowing down to you" (no. 12, § 1 and no. 13, § 2), there is no reason to suppose that someone else performed the praying in the name of the king. The description in no. 3, where both the king and his servant perform rituals, fully confirms this observation.

The clearest reference to the king's direct involvement in the recording of a prayer is found in the colophon of Muwatalli's prayer concerning Kummanni (no. 19), but unfortunately the key expression is broken away: "One tablet of the presentation of the plea to the Storm-god, written down [from the mouth(?)] of His Majesty. Complete. Written by the hand of Lurma-ziti, junior incantation priest, apprentice [of . . .], son of Aki-Tessub." However, the restoration is very plausible, and it shows that the prayer was taken down verbally from the king's mouth, or at least he gave general instructions and approved the final version.

"The Prosecution": The Offended God(s)

As a rule, every human sin is an offense against the divine world, but apparently there is a specific god who carries the complaint to the assembly of gods. The identity of this angry god of heaven or earth is usually not known to the suppliant, and the all-knowing Sun-god is invoked to find him and to intercede on the suppliant's behalf. In the prayer of Kantuzzili the angry god appears to be, as in Babylonian prototypes (Güterbock 1958: 242), the suppliant's personal god, who had raised him and supported him until now (no. 4a, § 1'–2'). In Puduhepa's Prayer (no. 22, § 8") the malefactor who defamed Hattusili and caused his sickness could also be a human, not only one of the Upper (Heaven) or Lower (Earth) gods. As in a court case, the prosecutor first speaks about the evil matter, and then the intercessor transmits the prayer of defense (no. 21, § 11'). Interestingly, in his prayer concerning the cult of Kummanni (no. 19), Muwatalli considers, among other evils, also the possibility that some local deity caused the Storm-god's anger (§ 2). In such a case humans are unable to help, and the gods of the Netherworld (*Anunnaki*) are asked to reconcile the Storm-god to that deity.

"The Defense": The Interceding Gods

In principle, all the gods addressed in prayers may be considered as intercessors transmitting the king's plea to the assembly of gods convened in Hattusa (no. 21, § 11'). However, the most frequently addressed gods, the Sun and the Storm deities, also preside at the divine court, and thus the distinction between intercessor and supreme judge is less manifest. Even so, their role as advocates of the defendant in the divine court is quite evident, for example in Hattusili's prayer, in which the Sun-goddess of Arinna and the Storm-god of Hatti are solicited to take up the king's cause in the assembly for the sake of their son, the Storm-god of Nerik (no. 21, § 11').

By far the most frequently addressed gods in Hittite prayers are the solar deities in their various hypostases: the Sun-goddess of the Netherworld (no. 1), the Sun-god of Heaven (nos. 4a–c), and, first and foremost, the Sun-goddess of Arinna (nos. 3, 5, 7, 8, 10, 16, 21, 22, 24). One prayer (no. 2) is addressed to the Sun-god and the Storm-god in tandem. The reason for the solar deity's predominance is obvious.[8] Not only is the Sun-goddess of Arinna one of the two principal deities of the Hittite pantheon, but the all-seeing and impartial Sun is universally considered as the supreme deity of justice, who in his circular daily journey meets all the gods of heaven and earth and convenes them to the divine assembly.

Typical for the Hittite Sun-deity is his concern not only for all human beings, including the evil, the lonely and the oppressed (no. 4b, §§ 8', 10'= no. 4c, §§ 4, 5), but also for the lowest creatures, such as the dog, the pig, the beast of the field (no. 20, § 66), and "the animals who do not speak with their mouth" (no. 4b, § 10' = no. 4c, § 5).

The Storm-god is also represented in several hypostases. In the Hurrian prayer of Taduhepa (no. 6) he must be Tessub. Mursili's "Second" Plague Prayer (no. 11) is addressed to the Storm-god of Hatti, the guarantor of the treaty between Hatti and Egypt. Muwatalli addresses his own celestial Storm-god of Lightning in no. 20, and perhaps also in no. 19 (Singer 1996: 161f.).

Other gods addressed in prayers are Telipinu (no. 9), the Storm-god of Nerik (no. 23), and Lelwani, who is invoked in cases of grave illness (no. 15; no. 22, §§ 8"–9"). An idiosyncracy of Hittite prayers are the intercessions of divine acolytes, who are asked to mediate between the suppliant and the supreme deity to whose circle they belong (Güterbock 1958: 242; Houwink ten Cate 1969: 88). In no. 1 the large entourage of the Sun-goddess of the Netherworld is invoked. In no. 19 Muwatalli invokes several Kizzuwatnean deities to dispel the Storm-god's anger. In no. 20 the same king invokes the bull Seri, the Sun-god of Heaven, and the Storm-god of Lightning, dedicating to each of them a separate hymn. In her prayer to the Sun-goddess of Arinna (no. 22) Puduhepa appends separate invocations to Lelwani, Zintuhi, Mezzulla, and the Storm-god of Zippalanda, vowing to give them presents if her husband is cured.

The prayers addressed to the assembly of gods in its entirety constitute a special category within the genre of Hittite prayers (Houwink ten Cate 1987; Singer 1996: Ch. VIII). The rationale behind this exceptional form of imploring the divine world seems to be a failure to receive the hoped-for response from previously addressed individual deities (Singer 1996: 151). In this typically systematic Hittite approach, the desperate suppliant turns to the entire pantheon in a last effort to reach out to even the remotest of deities who might have caused the calamity. Mursili addressed two of his plague prayers to the assembly of gods, one arranged "geographically" by local gods (no. 13), the other "typologically" by categories of deities (no. 14). The full development of the type is represented by Muwatalli's model prayer (no. 20), in which he addresses by name no less than 140 local deities. After the religious counter-reform of Hattusili and Puduhepa, this special type of prayer seems to have disappeared.

The Defendant Pleads His Case, or,
How to Persuade a Hittite God

A priori, the pleading king assumes responsibility for any sin committed by him, by his predecessors, or by his subjects. A total denial of guilt is impossible in a divine court. Having said that, the possibilities of exculpation, self-justification, even protestation against unfair punishment, are remarkably manifold in Hittite prayers.

The reasons for divine wrath are disclosed through various methods of divination. The discovered sin is regarded as a collective burden on the entire Hittite society. It threatens to exact its heavy toll of punishment until it is fully confessed and propitiated. The sins of a king, even a deceased one, may bring calamity upon the entire land, and vice versa, the sins of the population may fatally affect the king himself (Furlani 1934: 37). In the oracular inquiries of Mursili and his successors responsibility for the sins is often attributed to the father and/or the forefathers of the suppliant. Suppiluliuma's sins revealed in the plague prayers (nos. 8–14) are particularly heavy (murder of Tudhaliya the Younger; transgression against the oath with Egypt; neglect of the offerings to the Mala River), but Mursili, Muwatalli, and Hattusili also get their fair share in texts written by their successors (trial of Tawannanna; trial of Danuhepa; deposition of Urhi-Tessub, respectively). Mursili and Hattusili both refer to their young age and ignorance when the respective sins were committed (no. 14, § 12' and no. 21, § 2, respectively), but the former also acknowledges that "the father's sin comes upon his son, and so the sin of my father came upon me too. It is so. We have done it" (no. 11, § 8). Forgiveness is then demanded from the gods, just as a servant who confesses his sin is forgiven by his master (no. 11, § 9). Another recurring argument is that the persons who committed the sins have already died (no. 12, § 8; no. 21, §§ 2, 4'), and their sins have long been avenged many times over (no. 11, § 9). Hattusili even goes so far as to protest against the protraction of such old sins, committed by others, to his own days. This is simply "not right," he audaciously claims (no. 21, §§ 2, 4'), using an expression freighted with ethical connotations (see Cohen 1997; 2002).

Having exhausted the *non mea culpa* arguments, the defendant tries to minimize the gravity of his own sins. Muwatalli reminds his god that "since we are only human" some offending words may have come out from his mouth unintentionally (no. 19, § 12'; cf. also no. 20, § 4). These evil words are stored somewhere in the dark earth, and the gods of the

Netherworld should find them and dispel them (ibid.). Puduhepa solicits help for her ailing husband by quoting the saying that "to a woman of the birthstool the deity yields her wish" (no. 22, §§ 6, 15"). Another recurring motif is that of the "orphan king" who implores the gods to become his parents (no. 2, § 2; no. 4c, § 17; cf. also § 24).

The "moral arguments" listed above seek to arouse the gods' empathy for their excessively suffering servant. An entirely different rationale is subsumed in the "beneficial arguments," by which the suppliant tries to demonstrate to his gods that it is in their best interest to put an end to the misery of the king and his people. This line of defense takes up proportionately more space in the texts, showing perhaps that the Hittites thought that, after all, even gods would more willingly act out of self-interest than out of mercy for their servants. The ravages caused by the Kaska tribesmen to Hittite cult centers in the north are described at length in the prayer of Arnuwanda and Asmunikal (no. 5), whereas Mursili's plague prayers lay the emphasis on the decimation of the cult personnel (nos. 8–14). The gods are simply requested to realize that if the disastrous situation continues there will be nobody left to prepare their sacrificial bread and libations. Closely related is the "only in Hatti" motif, whereby the gods are persuaded that in no other land would they be so generously treated as in their own "homeland" (no. 5, §§ 2'ff.; no. 8, §§ 2f.). The most "personal" argument of this kind is found in Hattusili's and Puduhepa's insistence on their dedication to the Storm-god of Nerik and his cult-places (nos. 21–22). They expect compensation from the young god's parents, the Sun-goddess of Arinna and the Storm-god of Hatti, just as a wetnurse would get her reward from the parents of a child that she had brought up (no. 21, § 9').

The ultimate modus of the *do ut des* principle is the conditional vowing of presents. In most prayers the reward promised to the gods if they respond to the suppliant's wishes is just a better execution of the prescribed rites, along with constant praise and adulation (e.g., no. 12, §§ 7–8). Puduhepa, however, vows specific cult objects to the gods addressed in her prayer if they keep Hattusili alive (no. 22): for Lelwani a full-size silver and gold effigy of Hattusili (§ 9"); a [great] ornament for Zintuhi (§ 12"); an endowment of [towns?] with their inhabitants for Mezzulla (§ 14"); and a golden shield weighing two minas for the Storm-god of Zippalanda (§ 16"). Her son Tudhaliya vows to build a temple for the Sun-goddess of Arinna in her town, if he returns victorious from the battlefield (no. 24, § 2').

The Ritual Context

A description of the ceremonies and rituals performed in conjunction with praying is rarely preserved in the Hittite texts. The general assumption is that even when there is no clear indication to this effect, the presentation of the prayer was always embedded in a ritual of offering ceremonies (Houwink ten Cate 1969: 87). This shortage in textual data, coupled with the lack of pictorial evidence, enhances the importance of the two extant descriptions: in Muwatalli's prayer to the assembly of gods (no. 20; Singer 1996: Ch. IX), and in an early incantation to the Sun-goddess of Arinna (no. 3).

In both prayers the action takes place at daybreak on the roof. Muwatalli's prayer does not specify on which roof (no. 20, § 1). In no. 3 the king goes with his servant to the sacred *salimani* at daybreak, and the ritual ends on the roof of the temple of the Sun-goddess of Arinna (§§ 12"–13"). In both prayers the supplicant faces the rising sun, and no. 3, § 1 even specifies that the prayer must be performed on a clear day. One should not generalize from two examples for the entire corpus, but the close parallel between the only preserved rituals is noteworthy, especially in view of the fact that Muwatalli's prayer is not specifically addressed to a solar deity. As the sun rises, the king performs the libations and the breaking of the bread, and then says his prayer. Muwatalli's prayer provides detailed data on the kind and the quantity of offerings presented to each deity (or group of deities) on two wickerwork offering tables set up on the roof (Singer 1996: 156). Eventually, the offerings are burnt on two fireplaces of wood.

The Muwatalli prayer does not refer to other participants in the ceremony, but no. 3, § 2 specifies that "nobody should bow down and nobody should say anything," obviously referring to some audience. The same emerges from two parallel prayers of Mursili which conclude with the statement: "And the congregation cries out 'So be it!'" Perhaps the list of governors appended to some copies of the prayer of Arnuwanda and Asmunikal (no. 5) is also relevant to the question of the audience present at the recitation of royal prayers.

There is rarely any indication regarding the city in which a praying ceremony was performed, but the obvious assumption is that usually the king prayed in the capital. According to the colophon of no. 8 the scribe reciting the prayer on behalf of Mursili invoked the Sun-goddess of

Arinna for seven days in Hattusa and for seven days in Arinna. In no. 7 (which served as a prototype for no. 8) the fragmentary colophon refers to Arinna, Zi[ppalanda], and a third, unpreserved name (Hattusa?). The prayer recorded in no. 8 was recited for two weeks, whereas in no. 9 no time limitation is indicated: "When the scribe presents daily a plea on behalf of the king before Telipinu."

The posture and gestures of the suppliant can only be glimpsed through textual references, which use in connection with praying the verbs "raise the hands," "bow" or "kneel down." None of the pictorial representations of the Hittite royal pair can specifically be associated with a praying ceremony (as claimed by Furlani /Otten 1957–1971: 171), though the presentation of sacrificial offerings is often portrayed in Hittite reliefs.

The Evolution of the Hittite Prayer

Short spells and requests for blessings pronounced by an officiating priest on behalf of the royal family are already embedded within Old Hittite magical rituals and festival texts. For example, the following incantations appear in the ritual for the purification of the royal couple (Otten/ Souček 1969: 22–31): "Mercy, O gods! I have hereby removed the impurities of the king, the queen and the people of Hatti. . . . Just as the Sun-god and the Storm-god are everlasting, so let the king, the queen and the children be everlasting!" Such prayerlike passages, which belong to the Old Anatolian cult layer (Popko 1995: 81f.), are occasionally found also in Hattian (Klinger 1996: 738f.) and Luwian (Starke 1990: 519f.) rituals.

The short Old Hittite requests for blessings developed into larger invocations requesting the god(s) to protect the king from perjury (nos. 1–2) or to grant him success and victory on the battlefield (no. 3). These are rather general requests of well-being, still lacking reference to some concrete occasion, as is typical for later personal prayers. The exact date of these early invocations is difficult to establish. They contain typical Old Hittite linguistic elements, but the extant copies exhibit only Middle or Late Hittite scripts.

The first Hittite prayers attributed to specific persons are those of Kantuzzili (no. 4a), Arnuwanda and Asmunikal (no. 5), and Taduhepa (no. 6), all figures of the Early Hittite Empire in the first half of the 14th century B.C.E. In this period, characterized by a marked Hurrian influence (for example in Hurrian royal names), hymns and prayers written in Hurrian make their first appearance (Wilhelm 1991; 1994). It is difficult to indicate the source of these poorly understood compositions for lack of comparative material, but their origin may well have been in some northern Syrian or south(east)ern Anatolian region in which Hurrian was not only spoken but also written as a culture language (Wilhelm 1991: 40; cf. also Singer 1995: 126ff.). Kantuzzili, the high priest of Kizzuwatna, played a dominant role in the introduction of the new genre of personal prayer, which contains some of the most powerful imagery in Hittite literature (Singer 2002b).

No prayers of Suppiluliuma I, the great conqueror of the Hittite Empire, have so far been found. But his son Mursili II (c. 1321–1285), the most prolific of Hittite kings, has left us no fewer than a dozen prayers, two thirds of which are preoccupied with his plague- and enemy-oppressed kingdom (nos. 8–14), and one third of which deals with the tragic loss of his wife (nos. 15–18). Mursili's direct authorship has been questioned by some who deny the ability of kings to compose a text. But as pointedly phrased by Güterbock (1964: 111), "Mursili's personality speaks so vividly from the texts that go under his name that it is obvious that he must at least have given directions for their formulation, if he did not actually dictate them." This holds especially true for the prayers dealing with the sickness and death of Gassuliyawiya, which contain some of the most touching personal testimonies in Hittite literature. On the other hand, in some of the prayers dealing with the plague Mursili incorporated, almost verbatim, an older invocation to the Sun-goddess of Arinna (no. 7), which is itself an adaptation of a Babylonian hymn to Shamash.

From Muwatalli II (c. 1295–1272) we have two well-preserved prayers (nos. 19–20) and fragments of a third, which is not included in this volume (see Singer 1996: 165ff.). Although Muwatalli occasionally repeated metaphors from his father's prayers, his compositions are distinguished by originality and exhaustiveness.[9]

The usurper Hattusili "III" (c. 1267–1237), his queen Puduhepa, and their son Tudhaliya "IV" (c. 1237–1209) have left us three prayers (nos. 21–22, 24) and many fragments of others, three of which are included in this volume (no. 23). The closely related prayers of Hattusili and Puduhepa exhibit a highly intimate personal style, differing from that of their predecessors. No prayers have come down to us from the last king of the Hittite Empire, Suppiluliuma II.

The Prayers as a Source for
Hittite Religion, History, and Thought

Prayers are among the most personal and imaginative of Hittite texts, and thus provide various important insights into the intellectual world of Hittite royalty. Obviously, the best illuminated aspects are the various domains of religion, as shown in the following examples. The human-like nature of gods, both physical and mental, is particularly highlighted in prayers. The suppliant often refers to the eyes and the ears of a deity, but in no. 1, § 4' we also find a rare reference to the "thousand eyelashes" of the Sun-goddess of the Netherworld. "The innermost soul" (no. 4a, § 6') of the gods can at times be unforgiving and vengeful (e.g., no. 12, § 8), and at others merciful and well-disposed (no. 13, § 3). The latter is evident especially in the hoped for future and the idyllic past: "O gods, my lords! Since ages past you have been inclined towards [men] and have [not] abandoned mankind. And mankind [became] populous and your divine servants [were] numerous.". However, at present the gods irrationally decimate Hatti's population, eventually causing damage also to themselves. When nobody is left to serve them, they are bound to blame their victim Mursili (no. 10, § 3'): "Why [don't you give us] offering bread and libation?"

In most enumerations of deities the pantheon is divided into two "horizontal" moieties, gods and goddesses (see especially the long list of local gods in no. 20), and two "vertical" ones, gods of heaven and earth (or primeval gods), the latter called in no. 19, § 2 by their Mesopotamian designation (*Annunaki*). Both groups bow down when the Sun-god crosses "the gate of heaven" (no. 8, § 4) in his quadriga (no. 4c, § 6). A unique and enigmatic reference to the Sun-god arising from the sea is found in Muwatalli's great prayer (no. 20, § 66). Other deities are not as vividly described, but the prayer of Puduhepa contains the parade example of a theological syncretism: "In Hatti you gave yourself the name Sun-goddess of Arinna, but the land which you made, that of the cedar, there you gave yourself the name Hebat" (no. 22, § 2). The cult of the gods is described in much detail, aiming to demonstrate that in no other land would they be treated as well as in Hatti (e.g., no. 5, §§ 1ff.; no. 8, §§ 2ff.). Evidently, each king had his own favorite deities whom he more attentively served than the others, but, quite interestingly, Mursili claims to have a non-discriminating attitude: "When I celebrated the festivals, I busied myself for all the gods. I did not pick out any single temple" (no. 11, § 2). The ways befitting the virtuous observant are listed in Kantuzzili's exculpation: not to swear by god and then break his oath, not to eat sacrosanct food, not to expropriate an ox or a sheep of the gods, not to eat or drink without sharing (no. 4a, §§ 3'f.).

In the domain of black magic we have the grave, though somewhat obscure accusations of Mursili against his Babylonian stepmother, who allegedly killed his wife through sorcery (no. 17, §§ 3'-4'). The substitute ritual aimed at saving Gassuliyawiya (no. 15) closely resembles the ritual for the installation of a substitute king (Kümmel 1967). The angry gods are evoked by aromatic substances to return to their abode from wherever they are: in heaven among the gods, in the sea, in the mountains, or in an enemy land (no. 8, § 1; no. 9, § 3). Methods of divination are listed in the infinite quest for the reason of the gods' wrath: seers, diviners, old women, augurs, "men of god" (prophets?), dreams and incubation (no. 4a, § 6'; no. 8, § 7; no. 11, § 11).

Generally speaking, prayers are seldom a major source for the reconstruction of history. Hittite prayers, however, because of their pragmatic character, contain important, sometimes even singular historical information. Besides the hymnic parts, much shorter than in other Near Eastern corpora, the Hittite prayer consists of a sincere "dialogue" between the suppliant and his god, in which he reports all his problems and fears. In that respect, a confession in a prayer is a more reliable source than the usual genres of historiographic writing, in which emphasis is laid on success rather than failure, on praiseworthy deeds rather than contemptible transgressions.

The prayer of Arnuwanda and Asmunikal provides the most detailed source for the deteriorating situation in the north, with a list of towns captured and ruined by the Kaska tribes, first and foremost Nerik (no. 5, §§ 28'ff.). A century later Hattusili describes in poetic terms how he lifted Nerik up "like a stone out of deep water," and how he rebuilt the revered city which nobody before him managed to liberate (no. 21, § 8'). Mursili II is no doubt the most important provider of historical data, from a rare reference to his illustrious namesake's conquest of Aleppo and Babylon (no. 8, § 8), down to the military difficulties of his own days (ibid.). Most important, however, are the facts he reveals about his father's reign. The circumstances of Suppiluliuma's usurpation of the throne, after the assassination of the legitimate heir, Tudhaliya the Younger, and the exile of his brothers to Alasiya (Cyprus), are recorded exclusively in one of the plague prayers (no. 12, § 3). Of utmost importance are also the data concerning Suppiluliuma's dealings with the Egyptians, which tally with the evidence recorded in the Deeds (see

Güterbock 1960; Bryce 1998: 192ff.). We hear about the Kurustamma Treaty, the Egyptian widow's letter, the murder of Suppiluliuma's son, the two attacks on Amqa led by the generals Lupakki and Tarhunta-zalma, and finally, the plague caused by the Egyptian prisoners (no. 11, §§ 4f.; no. 13, § 5; no. 14, §§ 11'ff.). As for Mursili's own reign, we learn mainly about his agitated relations with his devious step-mother (nos. 15–18), but an oblique reference to a solar eclipse in his tenth year (no. 17, § 7) may provide a valuable anchor for Hittite absolute chronology. The prayers of Hattusili and his wife are naturally preoccupied with the justification of his regime by highlighting his military and religious achievements in the north, primarily the liberation and restoration of Nerik (no. 21, §§ 8'ff.; no. 22, §§ 2ff.). However, Hattusili also refers to other important events, such as the controversial legal suits against Tawannanna (no. 21, § 2) and Danuhepa (§ 4'), and Muwatalli's transfer of the capital to Tarhuntassa (§ 3').

Last but not least, the corpus of Hittite prayers is perhaps the principal repository of Hittite contemplative thinking, particularly valuable in view of the conspicuous scarcity of Hittite wisdom literature (for which see Beckman 1997b, with bibliography). In face of military catastrophe, grave illness, or the death of a loved one, man disregards the conventional rules of prudent phrasing, and cries out from the bottom of his heart for deliverance and for a better comprehension of his world. We discover in these prayers many a moralistic reflection and poetical gem, often characterized by a deeply pessimistic concept of life.

Metaphors and similes draw from the observation of nature and everyday life: "As the snake does not [miss] its hole, may the evil word return to his own mouth" (no. 2, § 5'); "The bird takes refuge in the cage and it lives. I, too, have taken refuge with the Storm-god of Lightning and he has kept me alive" (no. 20, § 7¹; cf. no. 11, § 9); "Just as the Storm-god fills the mother's breast for our benefit, [so let . . .]. And just as we are satisfied with cold water, in this same way [let] the Stormgod, my lord, [give us(?)] water(?) [. . .]" (no. 19, § 12'); "Wherever I flow like water, I do not know my location. Like a boat, I do not know when will I arrive at land" (no. 4b, § 26"; cf. no. 4c, § 18); "As the rear wheel does not catch up with the front wheel, [let] the evil word likewise [not catch up with the king and the queen] (no. 2, § 6')"; "The merchant man holds the scales under the Sun and falsifies the scales. But I, what have I done to my god?" (no. 4b, § 16' = no. 4c, § 15).

Human suffering is portrayed in powerful words especially in Mursili's mourning of his wife (no. 18) and in the prayer of Kantuzzili to an angry god (no. 4a). In the latter we also encounter the cynical remark on the perfidious nature of men: "Do not denigrate my reputation in the presence of other humans. Those to whom I did good, none of them saves [me]" (no. 4a, § 12'). A daring protest against collective punishment of the good together with the evil appears in the prayers of Mursili (no 8, § 10) and Muwatalli (no. 19, §§ 6, 10). The helplessness of human beings vis-à-vis divine wrath is pointedly expressed by Mursili: "To mankind, our wisdom has been lost, and whatever we do right comes to nothing" (no. 8, § 7).

Finally, the basic human condition is epitomized in the following reminder to the immortal gods: "Life is bound up with death and death is bound up with life. A human does not live forever. The days of his life are counted. Even if a human lived forever, and evil sickness of man were to be present, would it not be a grievance for him?" (no. 4a, § 5').

Notes

1. Cf., e.g., Farber 1995: 1900 for the Mesopotamian magico-religious thought and terminology, which completely ignores the distinctions reflected in our definitions.

2. For Mesopotamia, see, e.g., Falkenstein/von Soden 1953; Seux 1976; Hecker 1989; Römer 1989; Edzard 1994. For Egypt, see e.g., Barucq/Daumas 1980; Assmann 1991.

3. Cf., e.g., Foster 1993: 39: "Hymns tend to be lyrical expression of praise, together with pleas for general well-being. Prayers tend to be petitions for personal well-being."

4. Note, e.g., that CTH 376 (*Hymne et prière de Mursili II à déesse d'Arinna*) lumps together plague prayers (A–E) and a prayer for the health of Gassuliyawiya (F). For a tentative reclassification of this entry, see Carruba 1983.

5. See, e.g., the sword dedicated by Tudhiliya to the Storm-god on the occasion of his victory over Assuwa (Ertekin/Ediz/Ünal 1993).

6. In any case, it hardly points to a "democratization" of Hittite prayers in the early empire, as claimed by Lebrun 1980: 419.

7. Whether the king could read or not is irrelevant. Even if he was illiterate, as some maintain (Güterbock 1964: 111), he could still recite his prayers, as any beliver can.

8. The predominance of solar deities is even more conspicuous in Egyptian prayers (Assmann 1991: 827).

9. I differ on this point from Güterbock (1958: 245), who maintained that "it is obvious that Muwatalli's prayer is much inferior to those of Kantuzzili and Mursili."

The Texts

I

Early Invocations

The three prayers in this chapter are only preserved in Middle or Late Hittite copies (or versions), but they exhibit linguistic and thematic features pointing to earlier origins. They all have in common the typical Old Anatolian rhetoric associated with the ideology of kingship (for which see, e.g., Kellerman 1978; Starke 1979; van den Hout 1998: 73ff.), and there are no signs yet of any significant Mesopotamian or Hurrian influences. The main gods of kingship are conjured to protect the king from perjury (nos. 1–2) or to grant him victory and success (no. 3). In all three texts the preamble is fragmentary or missing altogether, but it seems that these invocations are not attributed to a specific author as in the personal prayers which developed later (Singer 2002b). In many respects these prayers resemble Old Hittite festivals and rituals of the state cult, which also contain short requests for blessing of the royal couple (see Introduction).

No. 1
Invocation of the Sun-goddess of the Netherworld against Slander (CTH 371)

The power of the spoken word was highly regarded in Hittite society, especially that of the "evil word," which could harm its victim just as badly as physical injury. Ruling monarchs were particularly susceptible to the dangers of slander, defamation, and malicious gossip, and they did everything in their power to root out any signs of potential treason against the crown. Magical ritual was used extensively to prevent and to cure the bad effects of the "evil tongue" (Hutter 1988: 113; Haas 1994: 884ff.). Occasion to counteract defamation was surely not lacking in all periods, but there were several junctures in early Hittite history when a sense of insecurity and distrust showed itself more intensively, e.g., when Hattusili I denounced on his deathbed the disloyalty of his own wife and son (Sommer/Falkenstein 1938; Bryce 1998: 99f.).

This and the following invocation share much of their terminology with the ritual texts (Carruba 1983: 17f.). The text contains Old Hittite language forms (e.g., *takku* "if"), but the script of the single-column tablet is Middle Hittite.[1] From the beginning of the preserved part of the text only the end of a ritual offering is left. This was probably similar to those described at length in rituals to chthonic deities (CTH 447–449; Hutter 1988; 1991; Beckman 1990). The simple and repetitious invocation is pronounced by a male or female officiant on behalf of the king. The gender of the deity invoked is not disclosed in this text, but the Sun-deity of the Netherworld was identified with various chthonic goddesses ruling the Netherworld: Sumerian Ereshkigal, Akkadian Allatum, Hurrian Allani, and Hattic Estan (Laroche 1974: 184f.; Houwink ten Cate 1987: 15; Haas 1994: 420ff.). She is implored to disregard slanders directed against the king by members of his own family and associates. Besides the Sun-goddess of the Netherworld herself, the officiant also invokes her large entourage: her protective deity, her vizier, her servants, her two attendants (Darawa and Paraya), the chief of the dignitaries (lit. eunuchs), the chief of the cleaners (lit. barbers), and the deified courtyard (Hilassi). Each is offered food and drink and is asked to serve as intercessor between the king and the main goddess.

§1' (obv. 1'–2') [. . .] libates to the Sun-goddess of the Netherworld and to the gods and [says] these [words]:

§2' (obv. 3'–5') Mercy, [. . .] O Sun-goddess [of the Netherworld]! The king herewith invokes you personally and[. . .] he appeals on his behalf(?). He treated you as a god. [. . .] he caught. He kneels down to the earth.

§3' (obv. 6'–10') If his [father] defamed [him], do not listen to him. If [his] mother defamed [him], do not listen to her. If [his brother] defamed him, do not listen to him. If his sister defamed him, do not listen to her. If his in-law or his companion defamed him, do not listen to him.

§4' (obv. 11'–16') Incline your good eyes, lift your thousand eyelashes, and look kindly upon the king! Incline your ears and listen to the good word! [. . .] forth to your servant, free him [from evil] and establish him in a good place! May there [be] growth in the land! May it thrive and prosper, and for the gods may the offering bread and the wine libations multiply!

§5' (obv. 17'–21') Mercy, O Protective-god of the Sun-goddess of the Netherworld! May this[2] be yours and you keep eating and drinking! Mention the king favorably before the Sun-goddess of the Netherworld and pronounce the king's name favorably before the Sun-goddess of the Netherworld. [If] his father, his mother, his brother, his sister, his in-law or his companion defames [him], do not let him do so.[3]

§6' (obv. 22'–23') Mercy, O Vizier of the Sun-goddess of the Netherworld! May this be yours and you keep eating and drinking! And he repeats in the same way.

§7' (obv. 24'–26') Mercy, O servants of the Sun-goddess of the Netherworld who regularly put her to sleep and invigorate her.[4] May this be yours and you keep eating and drinking! And he repeats in the same way.

§8' (lower edge 27'–31') Mercy, O Darawa! May this be yours and you keep eating and drinking! Mention [the king favorably] before the Sun-goddess of the Netherworld. Pronounce the king's name [favorably before] the Sun-goddess of the Netherworld. [If] his father, his mother, his brother, his sister, [his in-law or his companion] defamed [him], do not let him do so.

§9' (rev. 32'–36') Mercy, O Paraya! May this be yours and you keep [eating and drinking]! [Mention] the king favorably before the Sun-goddess of the Netherworld. Pronounce the king's name favorably before the Sun-goddess of the Netherworld. [If] his father, his mother, his brother, his sister, his in-law or his companion defamed [him], do not let him do so.

§10' (rev. 37') Mercy, O Chief[5] of the eunuchs! May [this] be yours! Ditto.

§11' (rev. 38') Mercy, O Chief of the barbers! May this be [yours]! Ditto.

§12' (rev. 39') Mercy, O Hilassi! May this be yours! Ditto.

§13' (rev. 40'–43') When you (pl.) come, bring up well-being! May it thrive and prosper! May the words of the gods be performed in the future! As he performed for the Sun-goddess of the Netherworld, he will also perform for you (pl.). [Per]form(?) for [the Sun-goddess(?)] in the future, and for the days [. . .]

§14' (rev. 44'–47') Free him from evil and [. . .]! When you (pl.) come, let them [. . .] before them! Before the Sun-goddess of the Netherworld [. . .]. [Pronounce] the king's name favorably!

§15' (rev. 48'–50') [May] slander [never sit right with you(?)]! He [. . .] not [. . .]. Whose evil [. . .]

§16' (rev. 51'–52') The word [. . .] *The rest is broken.*

No. 2
Invocation of the Sun-god and
the Storm-god against Slander
(CTH 389.2)

As in the previous invocation, in this fragmentary text the king seeks divine intervention against those who spread malice against him before the gods. The joint invocation of the Sun and the Storm deities as the supreme gods of kingship is typical of Old Hittite rituals (Otten/Souček 1969; Kellerman 1978; Archi 1988: 13). The motif of the orphan king who implores the gods to be his parents is also found in no. 4b, §23". The simile of the wheels (§6') recurs in the Middle Hittite ritual of Hantitassu (KBo 11.14 ii 22ff.; Ünal 1996: 82). The simile comparing the evil words to a snake (§5') is so far unique, but the depiction of evil persons as snakes is typical of the Old Kingdom (Bryce 1998: 93). The word of the gods is compared to an iron peg, an implement which is used in rituals to "nail down" witchcraft and uncleanness (Engelhard 1970: 115ff.).

The text is preserved in two large and two smaller duplicates. The script of the larger, single-column, duplicates is late, but their language is definitely older (*CHD*, L–N: 219f.; van den Hout 1998: 74). The text begins with some ritual preparations (*B* obv. 1–12) during new moon (l. 4), probably performed by an officiating priest. It continues with the confession of the king (ll. 13–16). According to the colophon preserved on the left edge of copy *B* the text was contained on a single tablet.

§1 (A obv. 6') [. . .] O gods, absolve my/their sins!

§2 (obv. 7'–10') [. . .] he holds. [. . .] his brother [. . .]. [I] have no [father], I have no mother. You, O gods, are [my] father, [you are] my [mother]. You are (like) His Majesty (lit. My Sun) and I, I (am like) your subjects.[6]

§3 (obv. 11'–15') You alone, O gods, have put the kingship in my hand. Mine is the entire land and its [popula]tion and I govern it. He who is not respectful of the gods, or is not respectful [of the kingship(?)], I will smash him, and [. . .] him. [Whoever use] their evil mouth against me [before] the gods, [and whoever] carry [evil] in their lips,

§4 (obv. 16'–19') they scare [. . .] under the neck [. . .] they [. . .] and they keep cursing [. . .]. [. . .] listen [to me, have] mercy [. . .]. [. . .] to the king [. . .]

The rest of the obv. and the beginning of the rev. is almost entirely missing.

§5' (rev. 4'–9') O Sun-god and Storm-god! [Incline(?)] good eyes and regard the king and queen with favorable [eyes] and keep them alive! Whoever should henceforth carry to the lips of the gods an evil against the king, bring the evil word of the gods crashing down on his own head and his entourage(?). As the snake does not [miss(?)] its hole, may the evil word return to <his> own mouth.[7]

§6' (rev. 10'–12') As the rear wheel does not catch up with the front wheel, [let] the evil word likewise [not catch up with the king and the queen]. [. . .] Behold, the word of the gods is an iron peg. [. . .]. new moon [. . .] Let the great gods [. . .] be witnesses. [. . .] seals [it] with [the seal of] the Storm-god and the seal [of the Sun-god(?)]. Complete. (*B ; the rest of A is uninscribed.*)

No. 3
Invocation of the Sun-goddess of Arinna for the Protection of the Royal Couple (CTH 385.10)

The script of this invocation of the Sun-goddess of Arinna is late (duplicate A is slightly earlier than B; Archi 1988: 7), but its language draws from much older prototypes (e.g., gen. pl. *siunan*). The same applies to the rhetoric concerning the role of the *labarna* (title of the king) and the *tawannanna* (title of the queen), which echoes the Old Hittite ideology of kingship (Starke 1979: 81f.; Archi 1988: 15; Haas 1994: 430).

The text has the style and the form typical of the Old Hittite state cult, with the ritual part flanking the invocation of the Sun-goddess of Arinna. Its purpose is to ensure the general well-being and success of the royal couple, their offspring, and their land. The introduction of the Sun-god of Heaven in §8' should be credited to the late editing of the text, when the Anatolian Sun-goddess of Arinna was distinguished from the male Sun-god of Heaven who joined the Hittite pantheon through Syro-Mesopotamian mediation (Archi 1988: 11ff.; but cf. Popko 1995: 103). The ritual proceedings and the ensuing invocations are apparently performed in two localities: at daybreak in the sacred *salimani-* (an unidentified cultic location; *CHD*, S), and on the following morning on the roof of the temple of the Sun-goddess of Arinna (§§1–11" and §§12"f., respectively). From the second invocation only a few traces are preserved.

Preamble and Ritual Offerings

§1 (i 1–8) [These are the words of (?)] the priest of the Sun-goddess [of Arinna]: [In the dark(?)], on a day which is fair and there is no cloud [. . .], on that day I order my servant: "I am going to the sacred *salimani* and as soon I have washed myself, give me my festive garment right away! Furthermore, it should be ordered:

§2 (i 9–10) 'Nobody should bow down, and nobody should say anything!'"

§3 (i 11–16) When it gets light at daybreak, my servant goes down and brings up pure water with a jug. He puts it before the altar and he places three sacrificial thin breads behind the altar.

§4 (i 17–21) I step before the altar and libate three times from the jug before the altar. The deity washes its hands thoroughly,[8] and I wash off my hands.

The following two paragraphs are very fragmentary. Apparently the priest performs the ritual breaking of the bread and other preparatory rituals. The beginning of the hymn is missing.

Hymn to the Sun-goddess of Arinna

§5' (ii 1–3) [. . .] she provided the growth of [. . .], grain, vines, [. . .] down all generations.

§6' (ii 4–11) She gave them a battle-ready, valiant spear saying: "May the hostile foreign lands perish by the hand of the *labarna*, and let them take goods, silver and gold to Hattusa and Arinna, the cities of the gods!"

§7' (ii 12–15) May the land of Hatti graze abundantly(?) in the hand of the *labarna* and the *tawannanna*, and may it expand!

§8' (ii 16–26) Mercy, O Sun-god of Heaven, whose mind(?)[9] is brilliant(?), whose sunbeams are luminous. Protect in the future the *labarna*, your priest, and your *tawannanna*, your priestess, together with his sons and his grandsons! Rejuvenate them and make them eternal!

§9' (ii 27–36) Whoever are the *labarna*'s first-rank people—his favored great ones, his infantry, his chariotry and their property—keep them, the aforementioned, alive in the hand of the *labarna* and the *tawannanna*, O most vigorous Sun-goddess!

§10' (ii 37–41) Rejuvenate them and make them eternal! May the property of the *labarna*, the king, become more and more abundant!

The rest of obv. ii and the beginning of rev. iii are broken.

§11" (iii 5'–19') May the land of the *labarna* and his *tawannanna* succeed, and may it thrive and prosper! [. . .] May the *labarna*, the king, and the *tawannanna*, the queen, [. . .] the Sun [. . .] let them make the [. . .] its border![10] And it will come about that in Arinna your sacrificial bread [will be plenty(?)], and the totality of the libation wine [will be] sweet to you.

Concluding Ritual

§12" (iii 20'–25') When the king [. . .], the priest of the Sun-goddess of Arinna recites these words on the roof of the temple of the Sun-goddess as follows:

§13" (iii 26'–33) At daybreak the priest goes up in the temple of the Sun-goddess of Arinna and facing the Sun he recites as follows: "[. . .] up [. . .] O Sun-god of Heaven [. . .]"

End of rev. iii; rev. iv (containing the recitation of the priest) is almost entirely broken, except for the colophon (restored after §13").

Colophon

(11'–15') [When the king . . . , the priest of] the Sun-goddess of Arinna [recites] these [words on the roof of] the temple of the Sun-goddess, facing [the Sun]. Complete.

Notes

1. The fragment KBo 34.19, also written in a Middle Hittite ductus, contains a similar invocation of the Sun-godddess of the Netherworld. It could in fact be a duplicate or even join to *CTH* 371.

2. Probably to be read as *ki=ma*, here and in the following paragraphs (Hoffner; cf. also Christmann-Franck 1989: 41f.). Friedrich (1957: 223) saw a *di* sign, which he rendered as either DI, "justice" (see also Lebrun 1980: 87; Carruba 1983: 18; Ünal 1991: 794), of as SILIM, "well-being, prosperity" (see also Güterbock 1978: 128; *CHD* L–N: 262b).

3. Or: ". . . do not abandon him," referring (also in §§8', 9') to the king (*HED* vol. 4: 296).

4. Probably the metaphor refers to the sunset ("put to sleep") and the sunrise ("invigorate"). The two Hittite verbs sounded almost alike (*sasnuskatteni, tasnuskittani*), like a rhyming pair (Hoffner).

5. The determinative accompanying Chief is "god," rather than the usual "man." This is understandable since these high officials operate in the divine world.

6. Van den Hout 1998: 74 restores these lines as follows: "You, O Gods, (are) my father [and mother.] My Majesty's [lords] (are) you and I, your servant (!?) am I.

7. With a slight emendation if *issas* to *issa-si*, "to his mouth" (Hoffner).

8. The washing of cult statues is well attested, but here the reflexive particle points to the goddess herself as the subject of the sentence (Archi 1988: 26).

9. For the reading *istanzas-tis*, see *CHD*, L–N: 298.

10. The Sun seems to appear here in the meaning of one of the cardinal points (see Starke 1977: 96), rather than the Sun-goddess of Arinna. From Old Hittite parallels (Otten 1962: 165f.) one expects that the borders to be set by the royal pair should reach the sea, but the traces do not seem to support this restoration.

II

Early Empire Prayers

At the beginning of the 14th century B.C.E. a new era begins in Hittite history, which may best be designated as the Early Hittite Empire (also known as the Middle Hittite Kingdom). After a long period of weakness, the Hittites returned to the international scene thanks to Tudhaliya I's victories from northern Syria to western Anatolia (Bryce 1998: 131ff.). The annexation of Kizzuwatna, a hybrid Luwian-Hurrian zone in Cilicia, and the renewed contacts with other regions of Hurrian culture, led to a massive wave of Hurrian influence felt in various domains of Hittite culture (Wilhelm 1989: 49ff.; Popko 1995: 95ff.). The intellectual treasures of Mesopotamian culture were also eagerly adopted in Hatti, both directly or through Hurrian intermediation (Beckman 1983b; Singer 1995). Personal prayers make their first appearance in this period, both in Hittite (nos. 4–5) and in Hurrian (no. 6).

Soon after the glorious days of Tudhaliya I the fate of Hatti changed again and the situation deteriorated rapidly under the rule of Arnuwanda I and Queen Asmunikal. The Kaska tribes from the northern Pontic ranges overran many Hittite centers north of Hattusa, and in their despair the royal pair turned to the gods in prayer, stressing the grave consequences of the disaster for both the people and the gods of Hatti (no. 5). Apparently the gods remained unimpressed, for the military situation continued to deteriorate under the rule of Tudhaliya II, Suppiluliuma I's father. The enemies attacked the Hittite homeland from all directions, and according to a late retrospect, even the capital itself was burned down, probably by the Kaska. We may ascribe to this period a Hurrian prayer mentioninng Tasmi-Sarri (Tudhaliya II's Hurrian name) and his consort Taduhepa (no. 6). Although the exact contents of the prayer is still to be disclosed, several military terms may indicate that it includes requests for success on the battlefront.

No. 4
Prayers to the Sun-god
for Appeasing an Angry God
(CTH 372–374)

The parallel prayers nos. 4a–c (CTH 372–374) are addressed to an angry deity who is turning the suppliant's life into a misery for unknown reasons. The male Sun-god of Heaven, Istanu (for whom see Laroche 1974: 185; Kellerman 1978: 205-7; Houwink ten Cate 1987: 15; Haas 1994: 141f.), is implored to summon all the gods to an assembly and to transmit to them the suppliant's plea in a sympathetic way. The extant exemplars of the three parallel prayers are written in Middle or Late Hittite ductus, though their linguistic features may go back to earlier, yet unattested prototypes (Güterbock 1978: 129).

In the oldest of the three prayers (no. 4a) the suppliant is Kantuzzili, a Hittite prince, probably the son of Tudhaliya I and Nikalmati, who was appointed as priest of Tessub and Hebat in Kizzuwatna (Imparati 1979: 172f.; de Martino 1991: 12ff.; cf. Beal 1986: 436, n. 59; 1992: 320, n. 1225).[1] He is the author of several other religious texts, mostly from Kizzuwatna, including a Hurrian language invocation of Tessub and Hebat (CTH 784 = ChS I/1, no. 11). This is the only prayer in the entire corpus which is attributed to a person who was not a king or a queen, a fact which no doubt reflects Kantuzzili's role in the flowering of this literary genre in the Early Empire (Singer, 2002b).

In the second prayer (no. 4b) the suppliant is an unnamed king, and in the third (no. 4c), which contains the latest version, the prayer is attributed to "a mortal" (lit. "son of mankind"). This term may serve to emphasize the distinction between the divine addressee and the human addressor, rather than point towards authorship by a simple commoner (but cf. Lebrun 1980: 419). Note that in his prayer "the king" also refers to himself as a mortal (no. 4b, §13').

Although the close parallel between the three versions enables the restitution of fragmentary passages, there are sufficient divergences in composition and wording to justify separate translations. For a detailed comparison between the versions, see Marazzi/Nowicki 1978; for the dating, see Starke 1979: 63; Klinger/Neu 1990: 148f. Parts of this prayer also reappear in free usage in Mursili's prayers (especially in nos. 11–12).

The prayer opens with a long hymn of praise to the Sun-god, the lord of judgment, which is best preserved in no. 4c (§§1–8), is partly preserved in no. 4b (§§1–14), and is entirely lost in no. 4a. Its Babylonian background is most obvious in the naming of the Sun-god's parents (Sin/Enlil and Ningal; no. 4a, §8'; 4c, §3) and viziers (Bunene and Misharu; no. 4c, §7), but may surface in less conspicuous motifs as well, such as the feeding of the animals of the Sun-god's quadriga (no. 4c, §6; Haas 1994: 142, n. 207; Wilhelm 1994: 66). Fragments of a bilingual Sumerian-Akkadian hymn to Shamash, which may have served as a model for these prayers, were actually found in Hattusa (CTH 794; Cooper 1972: 71; Wilhelm, ibid.), but the composition as a whole is not found in Akkadian (Güterbock 1978: 132). Its Hittite author skillfully integrated the Babylonian motifs alongside local Anatolian ones, such as the Fears (*naḫsariattes*) and the Terrors (*weritemas*), the assistants of Istanu (no. 4b, §13' = 8, §6; Friedrich 1954–55; Wilhelm 1994: 66f.).

The plea following the hymn also includes parallels to Babylonian prayers, particularly to the "incantations for appeasing an angry god" (Lambert 1974; Güterbock 1974; 1978: 229; see also Gürke 2000). This part, deploring the suppliant's agony and fear of death, contains some of the most powerful imagery of personal piety in Hittite literature. Apparently, the immediate cause for the prayer is a serious illness, the nature of which was perhaps disclosed by the fragmentary §20 in no. 4c. The suppliant begs the angry god, whom he designates as his personal god, to relieve him from his suffering and to reveal the cause of anger either in a dream, or through divination by a seeress or a diviner (no. 4a, §6). In his defense he claims not to have transgressed against any religious taboos (no. 4c, §10).

No. 4a
Prayer of Kantuzzili
(CTH 373)

This version, the oldest of the three, is preserved in a single-column tablet written in a Middle Hittite ductus (Rüster 1972: p. X), and two smaller duplicates. The lost opening hymn can be supplemented from no. 4c.

Pleading before the Angry Deity

§1' (obv. 1'–5') [Whichever] deity became angry, that deity has turned aside his eyes elsewhere and does not permit Kantuzzili to act. Whether that deity is in heaven or whether he is in earth, you, O Istanu, shall go to him. Go, speak to that deity of mine [and tell him(?)]. Transmit the following words of Kantuzzili:

§2' (obv. 6'–10') My god, ever since my mother gave birth to me, you, my god, have raised me. Only you, my god, are [my name] and my reputation. You, [my god,] have joined me up with good people. To an influential (lit. strong) place you, my god, directed my doings. My god, you have called [me], Kantuzzili, the servant of your body and your soul. My god's mercy, which I have known since childhood, I know and [acknowledge] it.

§3' (obv. 11'–14') And the more I grew up,[2] the more I attested my god's mercy and wisdom in everything. Never did I swear by my god, and never did I then break the oath. What is holy to my god and is not right for me to eat, I have never eaten and I did not thereby defile my body.

§4' (obv. 15'–19') Never did I separate an ox from the pen, and never did I separate (lit. ditto) a sheep from the fold. I found myself bread, but I never ate it by myself; I found myself water, but I never drank it by myself.[3] Were I now to recover, would I not recover on account of you, O god? Were I to regain my strength, would I not regain my strength at your word, O god?

§5' (obv. 20'–23') Life is bound up with death and death is bound up with life. A human does not live forever. The days of his life are counted. Even if a human lived for ever, and evil sickness of man were to be present, would it not be a grievance for him?

§6' (obv. 24'–28') [Now] may my god open his innermost soul[4] to me with all his heart, and may he tell me my sins, so that I may acknowledge them. Either let my god speak to me in a dream, and may my god open his heart and tell [me] my sins so that I may acknowlege them. Or let a seeress tell it to me, [or] let a diviner of the Sun-god tell it to me from a liver. May my god open [his innermost soul] to me with all his heart, and may he tell me my sins so that I may acknowledge them.

§7' (obv. 29'–rev. 5) You, my god, return to me [reverence] and strength! [O Sun-god], you are [the shepherd of all] and your message is [sweet] to everyone. [My god who] was angry [at me] and rejected me, [may the same one consider] me again and keep [me] alive! My god who gave me sickness, may he [have] pity on me [again]. I have toiled and labored in the face [of sickness(?)], but I cannot any longer. Just as you have scraped [off . . .], you have turned [. . .].[5]

§8' (rev. 6–9) May [the god's anger(?)] again subside and may [. . .] . . . to his heart again. Establish again [. . . O Sun-god], most vigorous [son] of Sin and Ningal, [your beard is of lapis lazuli.] [I], Kantuzzili, your servant, [. . .] herewith call you [. . .] and say [to you]:

§9' (rev. 10–13) O Sun-god, my lord! I, Kantuzzili, herewith ask my god and may my [god] listen [to me]. What have I, Kantuzzili, ever done to my god and [in what have I sinned] against my god? You made me, you created me. But now, [what] have I, Kantuzzili, done to you? The merchant [man] holds the scales before the Sun and falsifies the scales. [But I,] what have I done [to] my god?

§10' (rev. 14–17) Because of the sickness my house has become a house of anguish, and because of the anguish my soul drips away from me to another place. I have become like one who is sick throughout the year. And now the sickness and the anguish have become too much for me, and I keep telling it to you, my god.

§11' (rev. 18–21) At night no sweet dream overtakes me on my bed and no favor is manifest to me. But now, my [god], harness together your strength and that of the Protective-deity. I never even inquired through a seeress whether you, my god, ordained an illness for me from the womb (lit. inside) of my mother.

§12' (rev. 22–26) Now I cry for mercy in the presence of my god. Hear me, my god! Do not make me one who is unwelcome at the king's gate. Do not denigrate my reputation in the presence of other humans. Those to whom I did good, none of them saves [me. You], my god, [are father and mother] to me. [Only you are my father] and my mother [. . .]. *The rest is broken.*

No. 4b
Prayer of a King
(CTH 374)

This version seems to be slightly later than the one attributed to Kantuzzili (no. 4a). It is preserved in several copies, some of which exhibit a Middle Hittite ductus (Güterbock 1980: 42). The mention of Arzawa as an enemy land (§28") fits the historical circumstances of Tudhaliya I's campaigns to western Anatolia (Bryce 1998: 133ff.). The beginning of the hymnic part is missing, but it should be similar to the beginning of no. 4c.

Hymn to the Sun-god

§1' (A obv. 1'–3') [O Sun-god, mighty king,] son of Ningal! [You are] establishing the law [and custom]. Throughout the land you, O Sun-god, are a favored god.

§2' (A obv. 4'–5') [A strong lordship] is given to you, O Sun-god. Father and mother of all [the dark lands] are you.

§3' (A obv. 6'–8') [Your father Enlil has put] the four corners of the land into your hand. You are the lord of judgment and in [the place of] judgment there is no [tiring of you].

§4' (B i 1'–2') Also among the primeval [gods] you, O Sun-god, are mighty.

§5' (B i 3'–5') [You,] O Sun-god, [set the offerings for the gods], and you set the shares of the [primeval gods].

§6' (A obv. 11'–12') The door [of heaven] they open only for you, O Sun-god, and only you, beloved Sun-god, pass through the gates of heaven.

§7' (A obv. 13'–15') The gods of heaven and earth are bowing down only to you. Whatever you say, O Sun-god, the gods are prostrating themselves only to you. [You], O Sun-god, [are father and mother] of the lonely and the bereaved person.

§8' (A obv. 16'–20') You, O Sun-god, restore the claims of the lonely and oppressed person. When the Sun-god rises from the sky at daybreak, the radiance of the Sun-god falls upon [all] the upper lands and lower lands.

§9' (A obv. 21') You, [O Sun-god], judge the case of the dog and the pig.

§10' (A obv. 22'–24') You also judge the case of the animals who do not speak with their mouth. You, O Sun-god, also judge the case of the bad and evil person.

§11' (A obv. 25'–26') A person at whom the gods are angry and whom they reject, you, O Sun-god, have pity on him again.

§12' (A obv. 27'–29') And me, [your servant(?)], you sustain, [and I keep offering] bread and [beer] to the Sun-god. [O Sun-god, hold] me, your just [servant], the king, [by the hand]!

§13' (A obv. 30'–B ii 3') [A human has heaped up grain for the Four (draft animals) whom you,] O Sun-god, have harnessed. [So let your Four eat!] And while your Four eat the grain, hail to you (lit. live!), O Sun-god! A human, your servant, herewith speaks a word to you and listens to your word. O Sun-god, mighty king! You stride through the four eternal corners. The Fears run on your right, the Terrors run on your left.

§14' (B ii 4'–6') Bunene, your vizier, is walking on your right and Misharu, your vizier, is walking on your left.

Pleading before the Angry Deity

§15' (A rev. 2'–8') I, the king, herewith prostrate myself to you and speak to you: Whichever deity gave me this sickness, whether that deity is in heaven or whether he is in earth, you, O Sun-god, shall go to him. Go and tell that deity: My god, what have I ever done to you and how have I sinned? My god, you created me, you made me, a human (lit. a son of mortality). But I, what have I done to my god?

§16' (rev. 9'–11') The merchant man holds the scales under the Sun and falsifies the scales. But I, what have I done to my god? I am anxious and my soul is flowing to another place.

§17' (rev. 12'–14') I have become like one who is sick throughout the year. The sickness has become too much for me, and I keep telling it to you, O Sun-god.

§18' (rev. 15'–17') At night no sweet [dream] overtakes me any longer on my bed and [no] favor is manifest to my fate.

§19' (rev. 18'–20') [. . .] The Protective-god and the Strength-god (*Annari*) do not [. . .] any longer as before. [I] never even [inquired] through a seeress [whether] you, my god, did not ordain well-being [for me] from the womb (lit. inside) of my mother.

§20' (rev. 21'–22') [Now] I cry for mercy [in the presence of my god]. Hear me, my god! I have become a [. . .] man and in the place of judgment [. . .].

§21' (rev. 23'–24') I made [a plea(?)]. [. . .] it back to me [. . .]. You, my god, are father [and mother to me]. *Broken.*

§22" (B iii 1'–4') *Too fragmentary for restoration.*

§23" (B iii 5'–8') I have no mother [and father]. You, my god, are like [a father and a mother] for me. Now I go days and nights sleepless from anguish.

§24" (B iii 9'–13') Save me and release me, who am like a man bound in sins. Hold me in a favorable place and haul me up from the sea.

§25" (B iii 14'–18') Like a crippled(?) man I have abandoned running and on the dark earth I no longer move about as before.

§26" (A rev. 5"–6") Wherever I flow like water, I do not know my location. Like a boat, I do not know when will I arrive at land.[6]

§27" (A rev. 7"–9") I cry out [my sickness]. My god, hold my hand and take care of my flourishing before [the gods]. For me [. . .] I keep speaking up(?).

§28″ (A rev. 10′″–13″) [. . . began] to reduce the land of Arzawa [. . .]. against [. . .] Broken.
§29′″ (B iv 1′–5′) [. . .] his eyes [. . .] with the eyes [. . .] he saves [. . .] a man [. . .]
§30′″ (B iv 6′–9′) [. . .] nothing [. . .] seven times the sin[7] [. . .]
§31′″ (B iv 10′–12′) [. . .] may he succeed [. . .]
§32′″ (B iv 13′–16′) [. . .] when [. . .] to them [. . .] End of column.

No. 4c
Prayer of a Mortal
(CTH 372)

This is the best preserved and the most "modernized" of the three versions. It is available in a relatively well-preserved single-column tablet full of erasures and corrections (join-sketch in Marazzi/Nowicki 1978: 259ff.), and in several later duplicates or parallel texts. The main variants are indicated in parentheses. The last paragraphs carry the prayer beyond the point where the other versions break off.

Hymn to the Sun-god

§1 (i 1–13) O Sun-god, my lord, just lord of judgment, king of heaven and earth! You are ruling the lands (var. adds: and setting the boundaries) and you are giving victory (var.: you are giving life in [the land(?)]). You are just and merciful. You act upon (var.: are listening to) invocations. You are merciful, O Sun-god, and you take pity. The just man is dear to you and you are exalting him. O Sun-god, most vigorous son of Ningal, your beard is of lapis lazuli. A human, your servant, herewith prostrates himself to you and says to you:

§2 (i 14–21) O Sun-god, in the circumference of heaven and earth you are the light. O Sun-god, mighty king, son of Ningal! You are establishing the custom and law of the lands. O Sun-god, mighty king! Among the gods you are favored. A strong lordship is given to you. A just lord of government are you. Father and mother of the dark lands are you.

§3 (i 22–31) O Sun-god, great king! Your father Enlil has put the four corners of the land into your hand. The lord of judgment are you and in the place of judgment there is no tiring of you. Also among the primeval gods you, O Sun-god, are mighty. You set the offerings for the gods, and you set the shares of the primeval gods. The door of heaven they open only for you, O Sun-god, and only you, beloved Sun-god, pass through the gates of heaven.

§4 (i 32–38) The gods of heaven are bowing down only to you, and the gods of earth are bowing down only to you. Whatever you say, O Sun-god, the gods are prostrating themselves only to you. You, O Sun-god, are father and mother of the oppressed and lonely (var. adds: bereaved) person. You, O Sun-god, restore the claims of the lonely and oppressed person.

§5 (i 39–51) When the Sun rises from the sky at daybreak, your <radiance>, O Sun-god, falls upon all the upper lands and lower lands. The case of the dog and the pig you judge. Also the case of the animals who do not speak with their mouth, that, too, you judge. Also the case of the bad and evil person you judge. A person at whom the gods are angry and whom they reject, you consider him again and you take pity on him. O Sun-god, sustain also this human, your servant, that he may proceed to offer bread and beer to the Sun-god. O Sun-god, hold him, your just servant, by the hand.

§6 (i 52–61) A human has heaped up grain for the Four (draft animals) whom you, O Sun-god, have harnessed. So let your Four eat! And while your Four eat the grain, hail to you (lit. live!), O Sun-god! A human, your servant, herewith speaks a word to you and listens to your word. O Sun-god, mighty king! You stride through the four eternal corners. The Fears run on your right, the Terrors run on your left.

§7 (i 62–68) The Harnessing-god (*Turesgala*) [. . .] from the sky [. . .] they gave. In heaven they made [. . .] this deity for the Sun-god. Bunene, your vizier, is walking on your right and Misharu, your vizier, is walking on your left. And you, O Sun-god, pass through the sky.

§8 (ii 1–15) You [allot] the upper (spheres) to the celestial gods, you allot the lower (spheres) in the dark earth to the primeval gods. The nether [world(?) . . .] the primeval gods of(?) the earth [. . .]. To you [the human is] hereby [prostrating himself(?). . .]. Sun-god [. . .] the gods [. . .]. That deity has turned aside his eyes elsewhere and does not permit the human to act. Whether that deity is in heaven or whether he is in earth, you, O Sun-god, shall go to him. Go, speak to that deity and [tell(?)] him. Transmit the following words of the human:

Pleading before the Angry God

§9 (ii 16–28) My god, ever since my mother gave birth to me, you, [my god,] have raised me. Only you, my god, have looked after me among people with regard to my name and [my] reputation. You, my god, have joined me up with good <people>. Through hardship and roughness(?)[8]

you, my god, directed my doings. My god, [you have] called me, a human, the servant of [your] body and your soul. My god's mercy which I have known since childhood, don't I know and don't I acknowledge it?[9] And the more [I grew up], the more I [attested] my god's wisdom [and mercy] in everything.

§10 (ii 29–39) Never [did I swear] by [my god, and never did I then break the] oath. [What is holy to my] god and is not right [for me to eat I have never eaten and I did not thereby defile my] body. [Never did I] separate an ox [from the pen, and never did I] separate [a sheep from the fold. I found myself] bread, [but I never ate it by myself; I found myself water, but I never drank it by myself.]

§11 (ii 40–50) Were I now [to recover, would I] not [recover on account of you, O god? Were I to regain my strength, would I not regain my strength] at your [word,] O god? Life is bound up [with death] and death [is bound up with life.] The life of men [is not eternal (?)]. A small place [. . .]. The days of his life [are counted.] Even if a human [lived forever, and evil sickness of man] were to be present, would [it not be a grievance for him]?

§12 (ii 51–59) Now may my [god open his heart and his soul] to me [with all his heart and tell] me my sins, so that I may know them. May] my god [speak to me in] a dream. [May my god open his heart and tell] me my sins [so that I may know them. Or let] a seeress [tell it to me, or let a diviner of the Sun-god tell it to me] from a liver. [May my god open his heart to me and his soul with] all [his heart and tell] me my sins [so that I may know] them.

§13 (ii 60–69) You, my god, return to me reverence [and] strength! O Sun-god, you are the shepherd of all and your message is sweet to everyone. My god who was angry [at me and] rejected [me], may the same one consider me again and keep me alive! My god who [gave] me [sickness, may he have] pity on me again.

The following three §§ are almost entirely lost. They are restored after no. 4a, §§7'–9'.

§14 [I have toiled and labored in the face of sickness(?), but] I cannot [any longer. Just as you have] scraped [off . . . you have turned . . . May the god's anger(?) again subside and may . . . to his heart again.] Establish [again. . . . O Sun-god, most vigorous son] of Sin and Ningal, your beard is of lapis lazuli. Where is [. . . I, a human, your servant, . . . am hereby calling you . . . and I am saying to you]:

§15 [O Sun-god, my lord! I, a human, hereby ask my god and may my god listen to me]. What have I, a human, [ever done to my god and in what have I sinned against my god? You made me, you created me. But now, what have I, a human, done to you? The merchant man holds the scales] under the Sun and falsifies the scales. [But I,] what [have I done to my god]?

§16 (iii 1'–4') Because of the sickness [my house has become a house of anguish]. I cannot [. . .]. [Because of the anguish] my soul drips away from me to] another [place.] At daytime [. . .]. I have become like the one whom sickness and anguish troubles throughout the year, and I keep telling it to you, my god.

§17 (iii 5'–26') At night no sweet dream overtakes me on my bed. My name does not manifest itself with favor, and the word of the Protective-deity[10] does not beget strength for me. I never even inquired through a seeress whether you, my god, ordained an illness for me from the womb (lit. inside) of my mother. Now I cry for mercy in the presence of my god. Hear me, my god! You have made me a man who is unwelcome at the king's gate. In the presence of people you have denigrated my reputation. Whoever I am dear to does not acquire a good reputation (lit. take a good name). You, [my] god, are for me the father and the mother [whom] I do not have, my god. Only you, my god, are like [a father and a mother] for me. [From anguish I go sleepless] days [and nights. Save me and release me. [. . .]me, my god [. . .]. . . .[11]

§18 (iii 27'–36') My god [. . .]. Wherever I flow [like water], I do not know [my location. Like a boat, I do not know when I will arrive at land], away from the river.[12] (*erased passage*) [I cry out my] sickness and anguish. [. . .] (*erased passage*) My god, [hold my hand . . .] (*erased passage*) May my god consider me favorably.

§19 (iii 37'–iv 1) I will praise you, my god, and to you [. . .] my year . . . . . . [. . .].[13] They started hitting me. [. . .] Your, my god's, wrath [. . .]. If you, my god, are [. . .] displeased with me, I, who am a man again [. . .]. Now, my god, the evil and the sickness [. . .], and set me in a favorable place.

§20 (iv 2–7) In sickness the pus(?)[14] of [. . .] . . . [. . .]. Be a support! [. . .] bring! . . . [. . .]. [. . .] them away for you [. . .] bring [. . .]. . . . [. . .] . . . in sickness, in . . . , fight. . . .

§21 (iv 8–10) O god, do not let bad days and bad nights get close to me, a bewildered man.

§22 (iv 11–18) Remove my offense and regard me, a human, with [favorable] eyes! [. . .] for me! [. . .] death(?) for me. [. . .] Sun-god [. . .] the sin which [. . .] He called it for me twice, thrice. The sin [. . .] remove!

§23 (iv 19–23) [. . .]may he succeed. [. . .] down/by [. . .] this for me

[. . .] May these words of [supplication] soothe you in your heart, my god, as with cool water.[15]

§24 (iv 24–28) Just as I was born from the womb (lit. inside) of my mother, O my god, put that same soul back into me! May the souls[16] of my father, mother and family (var. offspring) become your soul, O god, for me!

From the colophon only " [. . .] completed" *and* "forth" [. . .] *is left.*

No. 5
Prayer of Arnuwanda and Asmunikal to the Sun-goddess of Arinna about the Ravages of the Kaska
(CTH 375)

This prayer about the ravages inflicted by the unruly Kaska tribes upon the Hittite cult centers in the north thematically recalls Mesopotamian lamentations for destroyed cities, such as the Sumerian lamentation over the destruction of Ur (Cohen 1988), and the Book of Lamentations in the Hebrew Bible which deplores the destruction of Jerusalem. Unlike the Mesopotamian and Biblical parallels, which describe the disaster that befell the city in vivid poetic terms, the Hittite royal couple lays the emphasis on the harm caused to the gods themselves, whose cult had been drastically terminated. The list of elements composing this cult—temples, cult inventory, personnel, offerings and cult calendar—and the assertion that nowhere else are the gods of Hatti piously worshiped, recurs in Mursili's plague prayers which are thematically similar (e.g., no. 8, §§2–3). From all the lost territories the loss of Nerik was the most painful. Through humiliating accords with the Kaska leaders (CTH 137–140; Neu 1983; de Martino 1992) the Hittites tried to transfer the vital offerings from Hattusa and Hakpis to the Storm-god of Nerik, but the Kaska broke their oaths and seized the sacred consignments (§§28"ff.). At least five copies of the text are known, some of them written in Middle Hittite script. Several versions append to the prayer a list of northern towns with their governors (*tapariyales*). These were perhaps present at the ceremony in which the prayer was read out.

The Piety of the Hittites

§1 (2. i 1–4) [Thus says] His Majesty, Arnuwanda, Great King, and [Asmunikal, Great Queen]: [To] you, O Sun-goddess of Arinna, [and to you, O gods(?), this prayer(?)], which Arnuwanda [. . .]

§2' (1.A i 1'–5') Only Hatti is a true, pure land for you gods, and only in the land of Hatti do we repeatedly give you pure, great, fine sacrifices. Only in the land of Hatti do we establish respect for you gods.

§3' (1.A i 6'–8') Only you gods know by your divine spirit that no one had ever taken care of your temples as we have.

§4' (1.A i 9'–13') No [one] had ever shown more reverence to your [rites(?)]; no one had ever taken care of your divine goods—silver and gold rhyta, and garments—as we have.

§5' (1.A i 14'–18') Furthermore, your divine images of silver and gold, when anything had grown old on some god's body, or when any objects of the gods had grown old, no one had ever renewed them as we have.

§6' (1.A i 19'–23') Furthermore, no one had established such respect in the matter of the purity of the rituals (var.: recitations) for you; no one had set up for you like this the daily, the monthly and the annual seasonal rituals and festivals.

§7' (1 A i 24'–27') Furthermore, they used to oppress your servants and towns, O gods, by means of corvée duties; they would take your divine servants and maids and turn them into their own servants and maids.

§8" (1.B i 9–11) [For you, O gods,] I, Arnuanda, Great King, [and Asmunikal, Great Queen], [have shown] reverence in every respect.

§9" (1.B i 12–13) Only you [gods] know [by your divine spirit] about the offering bread and libations which they used to give [to you].

§10" (1.B i 14–17) [We,] Arnuanda, Great King, and Asmunikal, Great Queen, shall regularly present fat and fine [oxen] and sheep, fine offering bread and libations. *Few lines missing.*

The Ravages of the Kaska

§11" (1.A ii 4'–7') We shall surely continue to tell you gods how the enemies [attacked(?)] the land of Hatti, plundered the land, and took it away, [. . .] and we shall continually bring our case before you.

§12" (ii 8'–13') The lands that were supplying you, O gods of heaven, with offering bread, libations, and tribute, from some of them the priests, the priestesses, the holy priests, the anointed, the musicians, and the singers had gone, from others they carried off the tribute and the ritual objects of the gods.

§13" (ii 14'–17') From others they carried off the sun-discs and the lunulae of silver, gold, bronze and copper, the fine garments, robes and tunics of gown-fabric, the offering bread and the libations of the Sun-goddess of Arinna.

§14" (ii 18'-19') From others they drove away the sacrificial animals—fattened bulls, fattened cows, fattened sheep and fattened goats.

§15" (ii 20'-25') From the land of Nerik, from the land of Hursama, from the land of Kastama, from the land of Serisa, from the land of Himuwa, from the land of Taggasta, from the land of Kammama, from the land of Zalpuwa, from the land of Kapiruha, from the land of Hurna, from the land of Dankusna, from the land of Tapasawa, (var. adds: from the land of Kazza[pa]), from the land of Tarugga, from the land of Ilaluha, from the land of Zihhana, from the land of Sipidduwa, from the land of Washaya, from the land of Pataliya,

§16" (ii 26'-27') the temples which you, O gods, had in these lands, the Kaska-men have destroyed and they have smashed your images, O gods.

§17" (iii 1-3) They plundered silver and gold, rhyta and cups of silver, gold and copper, your objects of bronze, and your garments, and they divided them up among themselves.

§18" (iii 4-7) They divided up the priests, the holy priests, the priestesses, the anointed ones, the musicians, the singers, the cooks, the bakers, the plowmen, and the gardeners, and they made them their servants.

§19" (iii 8-11) They divided up your cattle and your sheep; they shared out your fallow lands, the source of the offering bread, and the vineyards, the source of the libations, and the Kaska-men took them for themselves.

§20" (iii 12-16) No one in those lands invokes your names anymore, O gods. No one presents to you the daily, the monthly, and the annual seasonal rituals. No one celebrates your festivals and ceremonies.

§21" (iii 17-20) Here, to Hatti, no one brings tribute and ritual objects anymore. The priests, the holy priests, the priestesses, the musicians and the singers no longer come from anywhere.

§22" (iii 21-27) No one brings sun discs and lunulae of silver, gold, bronze and copper, fine garments, robes and tunics of gown-fabric. No one [presents] offering bread and libations to you. [No one] drives up sacrificial animals—fattened bulls, fattened cows, fattened sheep and fattened goats.

Large gap partly bridged by C iii.

§23" (1.C iii 3'-4') [. . .] the pure priests [. . .]. Furthermore, [. . .]

§24" (1.C iii 5'-6') [. . .] the priestesses we celebrate [. . .] we [. . .]

§25" (1.C iii 7'-10') [We shall keep] calling out to you the names of the innocent lands—Kastama, Taggasta, Serissa, Tastaressa, Takkupsa, Kammama, Zalpuwa, Nerik.

§26" (1.C iii 11'-14') And even now, we, Arnuwanda, Great King,

[and] Asmunikal, Great Queen, have cared for you, O gods, and we kept invoking you, [O gods].

§26" (1.C iii 15'-17') The Kaska-men [. . .] to you, O gods, [. . .]

§27" (1.A iv 1-4) They came here to Hatti [. . .] they conquered Tuhasuna [. . .], they conquered Tahatariya, [. . .] they came near/under the gate and [. . .] Hum[. . .].

§28" (iv 5-10) And since we are respectful to the gods, we concern ourselves with the festivals of the gods. Since the Kaska-men have captured Nerik, we send offerings from Hatti to Hakmis for the Storm-god of Nerik and for the gods of Nerik: offering bread, libations, cattle and sheep.

§29" (iv 11-14) We summon the Kaska-men and give them gifts; we make them swear: "The offerings which we send to the Storm-god of Nerik, you keep watch over them and let no one attack them on their way!"

§30" (iv 15-19) They come, take the gifts and swear, but when they return they break the oaths and they despise your words, O gods, and they smash the seal of the oath of the Storm-god.

§31" (iv 20-25) They seize [. . .] in the land of [. . .], and they [. . .] the offerings of the Storm-god [of Nerik] — offering bread, libations, [cattle and sheep. The Kaska-] men [. . .] it to the Storm-god [of Nerik . . .

§32" (iv 26-29) In the land of Hatti [. . .

In duplicates B and D there follows a list of towns with their governors (tapariyales).

Colophon

(1.D iv 3'-5') Second tablet. When they speak concurrently [the plea(?)] before the gods, pertaining to the Sun-goddess of Arinna. Complete.

No. 6
Hurrian Prayer of Taduhepa to Tessub
for the Well-being of Tasmi-sarri
(CTH 777.8 = ChS I/1, no. 41)

Amongst the Hurrian language texts discovered at Boğazköy there are several which can probably be defined as prayers (Kammenhuber 1976:

173; Wilhelm 1991: 40ff.). Among these, the longest (273 lines) and best-preserved is KUB 32.19+ (Haas 1984: 215ff., no. 41; cf. also nos. 42 and 52), which seems to be written in a metric form (Wilhelm 1991: 43). Although our present knowledge of the Hurrian language does not permit even a tentative translation, several comprehensible phrases clearly speak for the identification of this text as a prayer addressed to the Hurrian Storm-god Tessub: "May the gods know . . ." (ii 8); "I will provide(?) you again, may the gods be favorable(?) towards me" (iii 55f.). The author is probably the mid-fourteenth-century Queen Taduhepa (Wilhelm 1991: 40ff.), the spouse of Tasmi-sarri/Tudhaliya II, Suppiluliuma I's father (Haas 1985: 272ff.; Dinçol et al. 1993: 101), who supplicates the god(s) in the first person: "Listen to me, to Taduhepa . . . !" (iii 63). Although the exact occasion of the prayer is not known, one may perhaps compare it with Puduhepa's prayer for the well-being of Hattusili written about a century later (no. 22).

The text opens with an invocation of Tessub, who bears the epithets "the great (divine) king of the gods." One of the passages, which includes the words "weapon," "armour," and *marianni-* charioteers, may contain a request for the military success of king Tasmi-sarri who is mentioned several times in the text. Another plea may be related to the mention together of a "deaf," a "blind," and a "dumb" person (i 19f.), but the context is not clear. Even more intriguing is the phrase "He did/does not sit on the throne" (iii 39), which may or may not be related to the "son" (i.e. "crown-prince" ?) mentioned several times in the text (Wilhelm 1991: 44). Future progress in the understanding of the Hurrian language will disclose the position of this and similar texts within the corpus of Anatolian prayers, and their possible relation to Mesopotamian prototypes .

No. 7
Prayer to the Sun-goddess of Arinna
Concerning Plague and Enemies
(CTH 376.C)

This tablet exhibits typical traits of Middle Hittite orthography and language (Carruba 1969: 247f., n. 40; 1983: 5; Güterbock 1978: 136), although the copy itself is probably later (see the comments of Gurney 1977b: 200 on Neu/Rüster 1975: 3-5). The mention of the Land of the Hurrian and of Kizzuwatna as separate geopolitical units also point towards a date preceeding Suppiluliuma I (Houwink ten Cate 1970: 68f.;

Carruba 1983: 80). Mursili incorporated this prayer into his long composition to the Sun-goddess (no. 8), and "modernized" its wording and contents. Since most of the earlier prayer is quoted more-or-less verbatim in Mursili's version (§§7–10), a separate translation of no. 7 is renounced, but its main variants are indicated there. The colophon (restored after the colophon of no. 8) probably refers to the scribe who wrote down the tablet:

(rev. 18–22) When [people are dying] in the land. His Majesty [entrusted(?)/ dictated(?)] to me the word/matter(?)[17] [. . .]. I went [and invoked] the gods [in Hattusa(?)], in Arinna, in Zi[ppalanda and in . . . (?), and I spoke] these words.
(rev. 23–24) [By the hand of (?)] *Zu-u-w*[*a*[18] . . .

Notes

1. He must probably be distinguished from an earlier Kantuzzili (apparently his grandfather), a military man who placed his son Tudhaliya I (Otten 2000) on the throne, after murdering Muwatalli I (Singer 2002b, with refs.).
2. So with Kühne 1978: 168. Cf., *CHD* L–N: 115a: "even when I grew up"; Beckman 1986: 28: "Ever since I was born."
3. For this meaning of Akkadian *aḫīti-ia* in Boğazköy passages, see Güterbock 1974: 325, n. 10. Other renderings employed are "indiscriminately" (Goetze 1950: 400); "secretly" (*CHD* L–N: 414b; cf. *CAD* A/A: 190, under *aḫītu*); and "without thinking" (Kühne 1978: 168 and n. 8).
4. Lit. "his innards and his soul." For this expression, see *HED* 1–2: 468; Catsanicos 1991: 10 n. 3.
5. Goetze 1950: 400b restores: "No sooner didst thou scrape [one thing evil] off [me], than thou broughtest back [another] in its stead."
6. Cf. no. 4b, §18. The parallel passage in the Akkadian "incantation for appeasing an angry god" has: "Like river water I do not know where I am going, like a boat I do not know at which quay I put in" (Lambert 1974: 279; Marazzi 1981: 28f.).
7. This paragraph may perhaps be restored after the Akkadian incantation which has: "Though my transgressions be seven, let your heart rest . . ." (Lambert 1974: 283; cf. also Foster 1993: 687).
8. *ḫaḫaratar* is perhaps the abstract quality "roughness," of *ḫaḫḫara-*, "rake," "threshing-field" (*HEG* Lfg. 1:122; *HED* vol. 1–2: 368; vol. 3: 5f.). The parallel passage in no. 4a, §2 has: "to a strong place you, my god, directed my doings."
9. An affirmative sentence in Kantuzzili's prayer (no. 4a, §2) turns here into a negative statement. Perhaps Puhvel (*HED* vol. 4: 43) is right when he renders this as a rhetorical question (but cf. Güterbock 1978: 133, Lebrun 1980: 104 and *CHD* L–N: 465).

10. "Protective-deity" (LAMA) seems to be erased on the tablet.

11. The fragmentary continuation in the join fragment KBo 38.165 (Košak 1998: 229) seems to differ from the parallel texts.

12. Cf. no 4a, §26".

13. The meaning of *hantes arissa* is not known.

14. Or some other exudate; see *CHD* L–N: 163, s.v. *mani-*. This and the following fragmentary words were inserted above the live.

15. Following Melchert 1977: 256.

16. ZI.ḪI.A (Otten 1958: 123f.; Güterbock 1978: 134), rather than MU.ḪI.A (Lebrun 1980 1980: 101). It is difficult to fathom the exact meaning of this sentence, but it may reflect the ancient belief that the personal god dwelt in the man's body, and it passed from the body of the father into the body of his son (Jacobsen 1976: 158f.).

17. The last preserved signs in line 19 could perhaps belong to *A-WA[-AT*. Lebrun's (1980: 164) restoration *Mur[sili* is certainly wrong.

18. A restoration *Kiz]zuwa[tna* is theoretically possible, but the spelling with a long *u* would be unusual (Neu/Rüster 1975: 4). Scribes named Zuwa and Zuwanni were active in the thirteenth century (ibid.), which may well be the date of this copy.

III

Mursili's Prayers Concerning Plague and Enemies

In the reign of Suppiluliuma I a virulent plague broke out in Hatti which decimated its population for more than two decades. Suppiluliuma himself and his eldest son Arnuwanda II apparently died of it, and the difficult task of investigating the reasons for the calamity and trying to put an end to it were left to the young king Mursili II. As the immediate cause of the plague Mursili pointed to an epidemic brought to Hatti by Egyptian captives carried off by Suppiluliuma from the battle-field of Amqa (no. 11, §§5, 9). Whether this contact indeed marked the outbreak of the epidemic in Hatti is hard to tell. In another prayer Mursili traces back Hatti's troubles, including the plague, to the days of his grandfather (no. 13, §3). Also, a similar prayer written in the Middle Hittite language (no. 7) already refers to *henkan,* and there are other thematic and linguistic indications pointing towards even earlier prototypes for Mursili's prayers (Carruba 1983). It is difficult to say whether these early forerunners were already obsessed with the disastrous effects of epidemics, since the Hittite word *henkan* (like its Akkadian counterpart *mūtānu*) also has the less restricted meaning of "death, death sentence, doom" (Archi 1978: 81f.; *HED* 3: 296ff.). At any rate, plagues are already attested in Anatolia in the Old Assyrian Colony period (Çeçen 1995), and are often mentioned in Late Bronze Age Syrian documents (Klengel 1999b).

Whether introduced by Egyptian prisoners or not, Mursili's "diagnosis" was considered to be merely the instrument of divine wrath. The "real" causes had to be discovered through a lengthy process of oracular consultation in which various sins weighing on the collective conscience were suggested to the gods who were expected to respond by divinatory means. The results pointed, without exception, towards various sins committed by the king's father, Suppiluliuma. According to one prayer (no. 11), the causes for the plague were discovered in two ancient tablets: the neglect of offerings to the Mala (Euphrates) River (§3), and the violation of the so-called Kurustama Treaty by two attacks on the land of Amqa on the northern frontier of the Egyptian Empire (§§4f.; cf. also no. 14, §§7ff.). In another prayer the grave breach of oath concerns Suppiluliuma's murder of the legitimate heir to the throne, Tudhaliya the Younger (no. 12, §§2f.). These confessions add invaluable historical information on the age of Suppiluliuma, which conforms to and complements other sources (Güterbock 1960). Although the responsibility for all these offenses against the gods is laid by Mursili upon his father, he accepts, somewhat reluctantly, that "the father's sin comes upon his son" (no. 11, §8). His begging for forgiveness rests on two arguments. The first is practical: If all the people of Hatti will perish in the pestilence, who will worship the gods (e.g., no. 10, §3')? The second is moral: Just as a servant who confesses his sin is forgiven by his master, the gods should forgive the sins admitted by their human servants (no. 11, §9). Mursili performs the appropriate propitiation rituals, and along with them, he addresses the gods directly or through priests in a series of dramatic prayers, among the most beautiful compositions in Hittite literature. Eventually, the plague must have subsided in Hatti, since the subject is not taken up in prayers composed after Mursili.

At least eight prayers dealing with "death" or "plague" are known, including the four which have come to be known as the Plague Prayers, *par excellence* (Goetze 1930). There are also smaller fragments which defy a safe attribution to one of these versions (e.g., KBo 14.75; Lebrun 1980: 229ff.), not to mention the various historical (del Monte 1993: 113f., with n. 147) and ritual texts referring to plagues (e.g., CTH 407 and CTH 716; Collins 1997: 161, 164; see also Archi 1978: 87ff.). The earliest prayer, dedicated to the Sun-goddess of Arinna (no. 7), is written in Middle Hittite and may have been composed before or during the reign of Suppiluliuma I. It was incorporated almost verbatim in an invocation of Mursili II (no. 8), which, on its part, shows similarities with other invocations of Mursili (nos. 10–11). The rest of the plague prayers are identified as pleas (*arkuwar*) either by their colophons or by their contents, and they lack an introductory hymn.

It has been attempted to establish the sequence of the Plague Prayers on the basis of a development in Mursili's approach toward collective punishment (Güterbock 1960: 61f.; 1964: 112; Houwink ten Cate 1969: 97f.)—from emphatic insistence on his own innocence (no. 12, §8; no.

11, §6), to acquiescent acceptance of the guilt of his father (no. 11, §§7ff.). However, on closer inspection this moral distinction is less evident in the prayers themselves, and besides, one may suggest other criteria for setting up a logical sequence. For example, one might assume that the general assembly of gods (similar to the lists of witness gods in state treaties; see Houwink ten Cate 1987), was only addressed after the prayers to the individual gods had failed to achieve their purpose (Singer 1996: 151). At present it seems best to admit that the order in which these prayers were composed is simply not known. Some contemporaneity may also be assumed since the prayers are addressed to different deities: the Sun-goddess of Arinna (nos. 8, 10), the Storm-god of Hatti (no. 11), Telipinu (no. 9), and the assembly of gods (nos. 12–14). For the sake of convenience, reference is also made in the titles to Goetze's sequence (1930).

The styles exhibited in these prayers vary from free use of existing prayer sections (in the invocations nos. 8–9), to original compositions which are almost free of such borrowings (in the pleas nos. 10–14). Most versions have come down to us in late copies from the 13th century, and only a few may be identified as original texts, usually written on single-column tablets.

No. 8
Mursili's Hymn and Prayer to the Sun-goddess of Arinna
(CTH 376.A)

In this invocation to the Sun-goddess of Arinna Mursili complains both about the terrible effects of the plague and about the hostility of various enemy lands: the recently subjected protectorates[1] of Mittanni and Arzawa (§7), and the smaller vassal states of the Kaska in the north and Arawanna, Kalasma, Lukka, and Pitassa in the west (§8). The description of the Kaska as "swineherds and weavers" is one of the rare ethnic descriptions in Hittite sources which may perhaps contain a pejorative intent. Comparing the present deplorable state of affairs to the glorious days of the past, Mursili refers to his illustrious namesake who smashed Aleppo and Babylon like a lion (§8).

In the opening hymn to the Sun-goddess of Arinna the scribes of Mursili adopted parts of an older hymn to the male Sun-god Istanu (nos. 4a–c), which in its turn was based on a Babylonian hymn to Shamash (Güterbock 1978: 131ff.; 1980). Among the expressions excluded from the oiginal hymn are those referring to the male character of the deity, such as his lapis lazuli beard, and his Babylonian origins: his parents, Sin/Enlil and Ningal, and his viziers, Bunene and Misharu. However, the scribes occasionally failed to emend "my lord" when referring to the Sun-goddess (§4).

The prayer itself was adopted almost verbatim from the partially preserved Early Imperial prayer to the Sun-goddess (no. 7), after "modernizing" its language and updating its contents by omitting Kizzuwatna, which by this time had become an integral part of the Hittite kingdom. Almost the entire prayer has been preserved in text A, and most of the lacunae may safely be restored from the duplicate fragments (Carruba 1983; Otten 1991: 109f.), as well as from the prayers to Istanu (nos. 4a–c), and from Mursili's prayer to Telipinu (no. 9). There is also a general resemblance to the prayer of Arnuwanda and Asmunikal (no. 5), especially in the paragraphs referring to the wrongdoings of the enemies (Carruba 1983: 14). Similar invocations are also recited in a festival celebrated by Mursili II in honor of the Sun-goddess of Arinna (Jakob-Rost 1997, no. 7; Pecchioli Daddi 2000). The protest against the indiscriminate punishment of the good ones with the evil ones makes here its first appearance (§10). Distantly echoing Abraham's haggling with God over the destiny of Sodom (Genesis 18), Mursili (and also his son Muwatalli in no. 19, §§6, 10) calls upon the gods to punish only the culpable town, house, or person, and not the entire land.

Invocation

§1 (E i 1–10; A i 1'–5') [O Sun-goddess of Arinna! A mighty and honored goddess are] you! Mursili, [the king, your servant,] sent me [(?)[2]] saying: "Go and say to my [lady, the Sun-goddess] of Arinna: "I shall invoke the Sun-goddess of [Arinna], my personal [goddess] (lit. of my head). [Whether] you, [O honored] Sun-goddess of Arinna, are above in heaven [among the gods], or in the sea, or gone to the mountains [. . .] to roam, or if you have gone to an enemy land [for battle], now let the sweet odor, the cedar and the oil summon you. Return to your] temple! [I am herewith invoking you] by means of offering bread [and libation]. [So] be pacified and listen [to what I say to you]!

Hymn

§2 (A i 6'–20') [You, O Sun-goddess of Arinna, are an honored] goddess. [To you, my goddess,] there are revered temples in Hatti, but in no other land are there [any] such for you. [Only in Hatti they] provide for [pure and holy] festivals and rituals for you, [but in no other land] do they provide any such [for you. Lofty temples adorned] with silver and gold [you have only in Hatti, and in no other land] is there anything for you. [Cups and rhyta of silver,] gold, and precious stones you have only in Hatti. Only in Hatti they celebrate festivals for you—the festival of the month], festivals throughout the course of the year, [autumn, winter] and spring, and the festivals of the sacrificial rituals. In no other land do they perform anything for you.

§3 (A i 21'–28') Your divinity, O Sun-goddess of Arinna, is honored only in Hatti. Only in Hatti is Mursili, the king, your servant, respectful to you. They perform fully substitute rites, rituals, and festivals for you, O Sun-goddess of Arinna. Everything they present to you is pure. Furthermore, the silver and gold in your temples is treated with reverence, and no one approaches it.

§4 (A i 29'- ii 2') You, O Sun-goddess of Arinna, are an honored goddess. Your name is honored among names, and your divinity is honored among gods. Furthermore, among the gods you are the most honored and the greatest.[3] There is no other god more honored or greater than you. You are the lord (*sic*) of just judgment. You control the kingship of heaven and earth. You set the borders of the lands. You listen to prayers. You, O Sun-goddess of Arinna, are a merciful goddess and you have pity. The divinely guided person is dear to you, O Sun-goddess of Arinna, and you, O Sun-goddess of Arinna, exalt him. Within the circumference of heaven and earth you, O Sun-goddess of Arinna, are the source of light. Throughout the lands you are a favored deity, and you are father and mother to all the lands. You are the divinely guided lord (*sic*) of judgment, and in the place of judgment there is no tiring of you. Also among the primeval gods you are favored. You, O Sun-goddess of Arinna, allot the sacrifices to the gods, and the share of the primeval gods you allot as well. They open up the door of heaven for you, and you cross the gate of heaven, O favored [Sun-goddess of Arinna]. The gods of heaven [and earth bow down to you], O Sun-goddess of Arinna. Whatever you say, O Sun-goddess of Arinna, [the gods] fall down before you, O Sun-goddess of Arinna.

Few lines missing to the end of col. i. The beginning of col. ii is completed by 544/u (Güterbock 1980). The line numeration of Lebrun 1980 is indicated in brackets..

§5 (A ii 1–9 [1'–2']) The person at whom the gods are angry and whom they reject, you, O Sun-goddess of Arinna, have pity on him! And now, sustain Mursili, the king, [your servant], and [take] Mursili, the king, your servant, by the hand! And to [the words] which Mursili, the king, keeps telling you, hold [your ear] and listen to them!

Pleading

§6 (A ii 10–17 [3'–10']) O gods, What is this that you have done? You have allowed a plague into Hatti, and the whole of Hatti is dying. No one prepares for you the offering bread and the libation anymore. The plowmen who used to work the fallow fields of the gods have died, so they do not work or reap the fields of the gods. The grinding women who used to make the offering bread for the gods have died, so they do not [make] the god's offering bread any longer.

§7 (A ii 18–44 [11'–37']) The cowherds and shepherds of the corrals and sheepfolds from which they used to select sacrificial cattle and sheep are dead, so that the corrals and sheepfolds are neglected. So it has come to pass that the offering bread, the libations, and the offering of animals have stopped. And you, O gods, proceed to hold the sin against us in that matter. To mankind, our[4] wisdom has been lost, and whatever we do right comes to nothing. O gods, whatever sin you perceive, either let a man of god come [and declare it], or let the old women, [the diviners, or the augurs establish it], or let ordinary persons see it in a dream. We shall stroke(?) by means of the thorns(?)/pins(?) of a *sarpa*.[5] O gods, [again] have pity on the land of Hatti. On the one hand it is oppressed with the plague, [and on the other] it is oppressed by hostility. The protectorates which are round about, Mittanni and [Arzawa],[6] are all in conflict, and they do not respect [the gods]. They have transgressed the oath of the gods, and they wish to despoil the temples of the gods.[7] May this become an additional (reason) for the gods' vengeance. Turn the plague, the hostility, the famine, and the severe fever towards Mittanni and Arzawa. Rested are the belligerent lands, but Hatti is a weary land. Unhitch the weary one, and hitch up the rested one.

§8 (A ii 45–55 [38'–48']) Moreover, those lands which belong to Hatti, the Kaska land—they were swineherds and weavers—Arawanna,

Kalasma, Lukka, and Pitassa, have declared themselves free from the Sun-goddess of Arinna. They discontinue (the payment of) their tributes and began to attack Hatti. In the past, Hatti, with the help of the Sun-goddess of Arinna, used to maul the surrounding lands like a lion. Moreover, Aleppo and Babylon which they destroyed, they took their goods—silver, gold, and gods—of all the lands, and they deposited it before the Sun-goddess of Arinna.

§9 (A ii 56–60 [49'–53']) But now, all the surrounding lands have begun to attack Hatti. Let this become a further reason for vengeance for the Sun-goddess of Arinna. Goddess, do not degrade your own name![8]

§10 (A ii 61–67 [54'–60']) Whoever is a cause of rage and anger to the gods, and whoever is not respectful to the gods, let not the good ones perish with the evil ones. Whether it is a single town, a single house, or a single person, O gods, destroy only that one! [Look upon] Hatti [with pity, and give the evil plague to other lands.]

Some ten lines to the end of col. ii are missing. They may be completed from the parallel prayer to Telipinu (no. 9, §§10–13).

§11' (A iii 1–44) [Some] wish [to burn down your temples]; others wish to take away your rhyta, [cups], and objects of [silver and gold]; others wish to lay waste your fields, your gardens, and your groves; others wish to capture your plowmen, gardeners, and grinding-women. To those enemy lands give severe fever, plague, and famine, O Sun-goddess of Arinna, my lady! And you yourself, O Sun-goddess of Arinna, let yourself be invoked! [. . . let] the oppressed become fit [again]. To Mursili, the king, and to the land of Hatti turn [with favour]! Grant to Mursili [and to the land of Hatti] life, health, [vigor, brightness of] spirit forever, and longevity!

Five destroyed lines which may be completed from the parallel prayer, no. 9, §14.

Grant forever growth of grain, [vines, fruit-trees(?), cattle], sheep, horses [. . .].

Six destroyed lines which may partly be restored from no. 9, §11:

[Give them a man's valiant,] battle-ready, divine weapon! Put beneath their feet the enemy lands, and [may they destroy them].

O Sun-goddess of Arinna, [have] pity on Hatti. [. . .]. [. . .] winds [. . .]. May the winds of prosperity come, [and may the land of Hatti grow and] prosper. And to you, O gods, your offering bread and your libations will be presented. And the congregation cries out: "[So be it]!"

Colophon

(A iv 1'–8') *Few lines missing.* . . .] to invoke [the Sun-goddess of Arinna . . .] I then recorded the words of the tablet. I have invoked the Sun-goddess of Arinna in Hattusa for seven days, and I have also invoked her for seven days in Arinna, and I spoke these words. There is in addition a separate tablet of the invocation.[9]

(E iv 2'–7') [. . .] "When [the people] of Hatti [. . .] are dying [. . .]"; Copy [tablet]: "When they invoke the Sun-goddess of Arinna [. . .], they speak [these words]."

No. 9
Mursili's Hymn and Prayer to Telipinu
(CTH 377)

This plea is very similar to the previous one, though somewhat shorter. Mursili is accompanied here by the queen and the royal princes, which may perhaps indicate a somewhat later composition (Carruba 1983: 12). The text is preserved in two copies.

Invocation

§1 (i 1–2) [This] tablet the scribe shall read out daily to the god and shall praise the god saying:

§2 (i 3–7) O Telipinu, a mighty and honored god are you! Mursili the king, your servant, sent me and your maid-servant the queen, they sent me, saying: "Go, invoke Telipinu, our lord, our personal god (lit. of our head) saying:"

§3 (i 8–10) Whether you, O honored Telipinu, are above in heaven among the gods, or in the sea, or gone to the mountains to roam, or if you have gone to an enemy land for battle,

§4 (i 11–17) now let the sweet odor, the cedar and the oil summon you. Return to your temple! I am herewith invoking you by means of offering bread and libation. So be pacified and let your ear be turned to what I say to you, O god, and listen to it!

Hymn

§5 (i 18–24) You, Telipinu, are an honored god. To you, my god, there are revered temples only in Hatti, but in no other land are there any such for you. Only in Hatti they provide for pure and holy festivals and rituals for you, but in no other land do they provide any such for you.

§6 (i 25-ii 2) Lofty temples adorned with silver and gold you have only in Hatti, and in no other land are there any such for you. [Cups] and rhyta of silver, gold, and precious stones you have only in Hatti.

§7 (ii 3–8) Only in Hatti they celebrate(!) festivals for you—the festival of the month, festivals throughout the course of the year, winter, spring and fall, and the festivals of the sacrificial rituals. In no other land do they perform anything for you.

§8 (ii 9–19) Your divinity, Telipinu, is honored [only in Hatti]. It is in the land of Hatti that Mursili, the king, your servant, the queen, your maid-servant, and the princes, your servants, are respectful to you. They perform fully your substitute rites, rituals, and festivals for you, O Telipinu. Everything they present to you is holy and pure. Furthermore, your rhyta, your cups and your objects in your temples are treated with reverence. [They are] counted over and no one approaches the objects.

§9 (ii 20–22) [You,] Telipinu, are an honored god. [Your] name is honored among names, [and your divinity] is honored among gods.

The rest of col. ii is broken off. It was probably similar, though shorter, than the parallel passage in the prayer to the Sun-goddess of Arinna (no. 8, §4–5).

Pleading

§10 (iii 2'–8') [. . . Turn] with benevolence toward [. . .]. O Telipinu, mighty god, keep alive the king, the queen and the princes, and give them life forever, health, longevity and vigor! [Give] them in their soul [gentleness(?)], radiance and joy!

§11 (iii 9'–15') Give them sons and daughters, grandchildren and great-grandchildren! Give them contentment(?) and obedience(?). Give them the growth of grain, vines, cattle, sheep and mankind. Give them a man's valiant, battle-ready, divine weapon! Put beneath their feet the enemy lands, and [may they destroy them].

§12 (iii 6–17) But from Hatti [drive out] the evil fever, plague, famine, and locusts.

§13 (iii 18-iv 8) The enemy lands which are quarrelling and at odds, some are not respectful to you, O Telipinu, or to the gods of Hatti; others wish to burn down your temples; others wish to take away your rhyta, cups, and objects of silver and gold; others wish to lay waste your fallow lands, vineyards, gardens and groves; others wish to capture your plowmen, vinedressers, gardeners and grinding-women. To those enemy lands give severe fever, plague, famine and locusts.

§14 (iv 9–18) Grant to the king, the queen, the princes and the land of Hatti life, health, vigor, longevity, and brightness of spirit forever! Grant forever growth of grain, vines, fruit-trees(?), cattle, sheep, goats, pigs, mules, asses (var.: horses), together with the beasts of the field, and mankind. May they grow! The rains [. . .]. May the winds of prosperity come, and in the land of Hatti may everything grow and prosper! And the congregation cries out: "So be it!"

Colophon

(iv 19–21) One tablet. Complete. When the scribe presents daily a plea on behalf of the king before Telipinu.

No. 10
Mursili's "Third" Plague Prayer
to the Sun-goddess of Arinna
(CTH 378.III)

This short prayer, like no. 8, is addressed to the Sun-goddess of Arinna, but is entirely different in character. It lacks an introductory hymn, and resembles the plague prayers addressed to other deities (nos. 13–15). The only innovative section, which provides a vivid picture of how fragile life could be in Hatti (§2), is unfortunately badly preserved. A confessed sin does not appear in the extant part of the text. Only one, single-column copy of the text has come down to us.

§1 (obv. 1–6) O Sun-goddess of Arinna, my lady! O gods, my lords! What is this [you have done]? You have allowed a plague into Hatti, so that Hatti has been badly oppressed [by the plague. People kept dying] at the time of my father, at the time of my brother, and now since I have become priest of the gods, they keep on dying [in my time]. For twenty years now people have been dying [in great numbers] in Hatti. Hatti [has been very badly damaged] by the plague.

§2 (obv. 7–13) Hatti has been very much oppressed by the plague. [If someone] produces a child, [the . . .] of the plague [snatches (?)] it from him. Should he reach adulthood, he will not attain old age. [And even if old age(?)] will be left for someone, he [will be oppressed(?) by] the plague. He will not [return] to his previous condition. When he reaches old age, [he will . . .], but he will not keep warm.

The rest of the obverse and a large portion of the reverse are lost.

§3' (rev. 2'–14') I, Mursili, [your priest, your servant,] hereby plead my case. Hear] me O gods, my lords! [Send away] the worry from my heart, [take away the anguish from my soul!] Let the plague [be removed] from Hatti, and send it to the enemy lands. In Hatti [. . .]. But if the gods, my lords, [do not remove] the plague [from Hatti], the makers of offering bread and the libation pourers will keep on dying. And if they too die, [the offering bread] and the libation will be cut off from the gods, my lords. Then you, O gods, [my lords], will proceed to hold the sin against me, saying: "Why [don't you give us] offering bread and libation?" May the gods, my lords, again have pity on Hatti, and send the plague away. [May the plague subside] in Hatti. May it thrive and grow and [return to] its previous condition.

No. 11
Mursili's "Second" Plague Prayer to the Storm-god of Hatti
(CTH 378.II)

This is the longest and the best-known plague prayer of Mursili, in which he reports the discovery of two ancient tablets, one dealing with the neglect of sacrifices due to the deified Mala (Euphrates) River (§3), the other with Suppiluliuma's breach of his treaty with the Egyptians and the dire consequences thereoff (§§4–5; Güterbock 1960). The text has been preserved in three late copies, of which A seems to be the oldest, preserving the original one-column format of its prototype.

§1 (C i 1–18) O Storm-god of Hatti, my lord! [O gods], my lords! Mursili, your servant, has sent me saying: "Go speak to the Storm-god of Hatti, my lord, and to the gods, my lords": What is this that you have done? You have allowed a plague into Hatti, so that Hatti has been very badly oppressed by the plague. People kept dying in the time of my father, in the time of my brother, and since I have become priest of the gods, they keep on dying in my time. For twenty years now people have been dying in Hatti. Will the plague never be removed from Hatti? I cannot control the worry of my heart, I can no longer control the anguish of my soul.

§2 (C i 19–28; A obv. 1'–5') When I celebrated the festivals, I busied myself for all the gods. I did not pick out any single temple. I have repeatedly pled to all the gods concerning the plague, and I have repeatedly made vows [to them] saying: "Listen [to me O gods], my [lords, and send away] the plague from Hatti. Hatti can [no longer bear this plague. Let the matter on account of which] it has been decimated [either be established through an oracle], or [let me see] it [in a dream, or let a man of god] declare [it]." But the gods [did not listen] to me, [and] the plague has not subsided in Hatti. [Hatti has been severely oppressed by the plague].

§3 (A obv. 6'–12') [The few] makers of offering bread [and libation pourers] of the gods who still remained died off. [The matter of the plague] continued to trouble [me, and I inquired about it] to the god [through an oracle]. [I found] two old tablets: one tablet dealt with [the ritual of the Mala River]. Earlier kings performed the ritual of the Mala River, but because [people have been dying] in Hatti since the days of my father, we never performed [the ritual] of the Mala River.

§4 (obv. 13'–24') The second tablet dealt with the town of Kurustamma: how the Storm-god of Hatti carried the men of Kurustamma to Egyptian territory and how the Storm-god of Hatti made a treaty between them and the men of Hatti, so that they were put under oath by the Storm-god of Hatti. Since the men of Hatti and the men of Egypt were bound by the oath of the Storm-god of Hatti, and the men of Hatti proceeded to get the upper hand, the men of Hatti thereby suddenly transgressed the oath of the gods. My father sent infantry and chariotry, and they attacked the borderland of Egypt, the land of Amqa. And again he sent, and again they attacked. When the men of Egypt became afraid, they came and asked my father outright for his son for kingship. But when my father gave them his son, as they led him off, they murdered him. My father was appalled and he went to Egyptian territory, attacked the Egyptians, and destroyed the Egyptian infantry and chariotry.

§5 (obv. 25'–34') At that time too the Storm-god of Hatti, my lord, by his verdict caused my father to prevail, and he defeated the infantry and the chariotry of Egypt and beat them. But when the prisoners of war who had been captured were led back to Hatti, a plague broke out among the prisoners of war, and [they began] to die. When the prisoners of war were carried off to Hatti, the prisoners of war brought the plague into Hatti. From that day on people have been dying in Hatti. When I found the aforementioned tablet dealing with Egypt, I inquired about it to the god through an oracle saying: "Has this matter been brought about by the Storm-god of Hatti because the men of Egypt and the men of Hatti had been put under oath by the Storm-god of Hatti?"

§6 (A obv. 35'–46'–C iii 3'–7') "And because the *damnassara*-deities were in the temple of the Storm-god, my lord, whereupon the men of Hatti themselves suddenly transgressed the word (of the oath), did this become the cause for the anger of the Storm-god of Hatti, my lord?" And it was confirmed by the oracle. Because of the plague I also asked the oracle about the ritual of the [Mala] River. And then too it was confirmed that I should appear before the Storm-god of Hatti, my lord. I have [just] confessed [the sin before the Storm-god of Hatti]. It is so. We have done [it. But the sin did not] take place in my time. [It took place] in the time of my father [. . .]. [. . . that] I know for certain [. . .]. [. . .] the matter. [But since] the Storm-god [of Hatti, my lord], is angry about [that matter, and] since people are dying in Hatti, [. . .] I will keep making [a plea] about it [to] the Storm-god of Hatti, my lord. I kneel down to you and cry for mercy. Hear me, O Storm-god of Hatti, my lord! May the plague be removed from Hatti.

§7 (C iii 8'–19'–B iii 16'–24')[10] I will keep removing the causes of the plague which have been established through oracle, and I will keep making restitution for them. With regard to the problem of the oath of the gods which was established as a cause for the plague, I have offered the ritual of the oath for the Storm-god of Hatti, [my lord]. I have also offered [to the gods, my lords]. [I have offered . . .] to you, Storm-god of Hatti [. . .], a ritual for you, [O gods . . .]. As for the [ritual] of the Mala River, which was established for me as a cause for the plague, since I am herewith on my way [to] the Mala River, forgive me, O Storm-god of Hatti, my lord, and O gods, my lords, for (neglecting) the ritual of the Mala River. I am going to perform the ritual of the Mala River, and I will carry it out. And as for the reason for which I am performing it, namely, because of the plague, have pity on me, O gods, my lords, and may the plague subside in Hatti.

§8 (A rev. 10'–19') O Storm-god of Hatti, my lord! O gods, my lords! So it happens that people always sin. My father sinned as well and he transgressed the word of the Storm-god of Hatti, my lord. But I did not sin in any way. Nevertheless, it so happens that the father's sin comes upon his son, and so the sin of my father came upon me too. I have just confessed it to the Storm-god of Hatti, my lord, and to the gods, my lords. It is so. We have done it. But because I have confessed the sin of my father, may the soul of the Storm-god of Hatti, my lord, and of the gods, my lords, be appeased again. May you again have pity on me, and send the plague away from Hatti. Let those few makers of offering bread and libation pourers who still remain not die on me.

§9 (rev. 20'–36') I am now continuing to make my plea to the Storm-god, my lord, concerning the plague. Hear me, O Storm-god, my lord, and save my life! [I say] to you [as follows]: The bird takes refuge in the cage, and the cage preserves its life.[11] Or if something bothers some servant and he makes a plea to his lord, his lord listens to him, [has pity] on him, and he sets right what was bothering him. Or if some servant has committed a sin, but he confesses the sin before his lord, his lord may do with him whatever he wishes; but since he has confessed his sin before his lord, his lord's soul is appeased, and the lord will not call that servant to account. I have confessed the sin of my father. It is so. I have done it. If there is some restitution (to be made), then there has already [been paid (?)] much for this plague [caused by (?)] the prisoners of war who were brought back from Egyptian territory and by the civilian captives who were brought back. [And] since Hatti has made restitution through the plague, it [has made restitution] for it twenty-fold. Indeed, it has already become that much. And yet the soul of the Storm-god of Hatti, my lord, and of all the gods, my lords, is not at all appeased. Or if you want to require from me some additional restitution, specify it to me in a dream, and I shall give it to you.

§10 (rev. 37'–40') I am now continuing to plead to the Storm-god of Hatti, my lord. Save my life! [And if] perhaps people have been dying for this reason, then during the time that I set it right, let there be no more deaths among those makers of offering bread and libation pourers to the gods who are still left.

§11 (A rev. 41'–44'–C iv 14'–22') [Or] if people have been dying because of some other reason, then let me either see it in a dream, or let it be established through an oracle, or let a man of god declare it, or, according to what I instructed all the priests, they shall regularly sleep holy.[12] O Storm-god of Hatti, save my life! Let the gods, my lords, show me their divine power! Let someone see it in a dream. Let the reason for which people have been dying be discovered. We shall stroke(?) by means of the pins(?) of a *sarpa*.[13] O Storm-god of Hatti, my lord, save my life, and may the plague be removed from Hatti.

Colophon

(C iv 23–25) One tablet, complete. [How] Mursili made [a plea] because of the plague [. . .].

No. 12
Mursili's "First" Plague Prayer
to the Assembly of Gods and Godesses
(CTH 378.I)

This prayer could represent a forerunner of the prayers to the Assembly of gods (nos. 13–14; Houwink ten Cate 1987; Singer 1996: 152). Mursili personally addresses the entire pantheon, divided into male and female deities, without listing their names as in later pleadings before the divine assembly. He describes an ideal situation in the days of his father, until the gods decide to revenge the blood of Tudhaliya the Younger, the legitimate heir to the throne, who was murdered by Suppiluliuma and his supporters (§4). No mention is made of the Egyptian captives as the cause of the plague. There are two extant exemplars of the text, a single-column tablet and a late double-column copy.

§1 (obv. 1–7) [All] you male [gods], all female gods [of heaven(?)], all male gods [of the oath], all female gods of the oath, [all] male primeval [gods], all female (primeval) gods, you gods who have been summoned to assembly for bearing witness to the oath on this [matter], mountains, rivers, springs, and underground watercourses. I, Mursili, [great king(?)], your priest, your servant, herewith plead with you. [Listen] to me O gods, my lords, in the matter in which I am making a plea to you!

§2 (obv. 8–15) O gods, [my] lords! A plague broke out in Hatti, and Hatti has been severely damaged by the plague. And since for twenty years now in Hatti people have been dying, the affair of Tudhaliya the Younger, son of Tudhaliya, started to weigh on [me]. I inquired about it to the god through an oracle, and the affair of Tudhaliya was confirmed by the deity. Since Tudhaliya the Younger was their lord in Hatti, the princes, the noblemen, the commanders of the thousands, the officers, [the corporals(?)][14] of Hatti and all [the infantry] and chariotry of Hatti swore an oath to him. My father also swore an oath to him.

§3 (obv. 16–22) [But when my father] wronged Tudhaliya, all [the princes, the noblemen], the commanders of the thousands, and the officers of Hatti [went over] to my father. The deities by whom the oath was sworn [seized] Tudhaliya and they killed [Tudhaliya]. Furthermore, they killed those of his brothers [who stood by] him. [. . .] they sent to Alasiya (Cyprus) and [. . .]. And [since Tudhaliya the Younger] was their [lord], they [. . .] to him [. . .]. [. . .] and the lords transgressed the oath [. . .].

§4 (obv. 23–40) [But, you, O gods], my [lords], protected my father. [. . .]. And because Hatti [was attacked(?)] by the [enemy, and the enemy] had taken [borderlands] of Hatti, [my father kept attacking the enemy lands] and kept defeating them. He took back the borderlands of Hatti, which [the enemy had taken] and [resettled] them. Furthermore, [he conquered] still other foreign lands [during his] kingship. He sustained Hatti and [secured] its borders on each side. During his reign the entire land of Hatti did well. [Men(?)], cattle and sheep became numerous in his days, and the civilian prisoners who [were brought] from the land of the enemy survived as well. Nothing perished. But now you, O gods, [my lords], have eventually taken vengeance on my father for this affair of Tudhaliya the Younger. My father [died(?)] because of the blood of Tudhaliya, and the princes, the noblemen, the commanders of the thousands, and the officers who went over [to my father], they also died because of [that] affair. This same affair also came upon the land of Hatti, and the population of the land of [Hatti] began to perish because of [this] affair. Until now Hatti [. . .], but now the plague [has become] even [worse]. Hatti has been [severely] damaged by the plague, and it has been decimated. I, Mursili, [your servant], cannot [overcome] the worry [of my heart], I can no longer [overcome] the anguish of my soul.

§5 (obv. 41–47) *Very fragmentary passage in which Mursili apparently continues to plead with the oath-deities concerning their vengeance of Tudhaliya's blood. About five more lines, which open a new paragraph, are missing from the end of the obverse. The first seven lines of the reverse, which may belong to the same paragraph, are also very fragmentary.*

§6 (rev. 8'–12') [Now,] I have confessed [it to you, O gods(?). Because] my father [killed (?)] Tudhaliya [and . . .], my father therefore [performed] a ritual (for the expiation) of blood. But [the land of] Hatti did not [perform] anything for itself. I performed [the ritual of the blood], but the land did not perform anything. They did nothing on behalf [of] the land.

§7 (rev. 13'–20') Now, because Hatti has been severely oppressed by the plague, and the population of Hatti continues to die, the affair of

Tudhaliya has troubled the land. It has been confirmed for me by [the god], and I have further investigated [it] by oracle. They are performing before you, [O gods], my lords, the ritual of the oath which was confirmed for you, [O gods], my lords, and for your temples, with regard to the plague of the land and they are clearing [it (i.e. the oath obligation) before] you. And I am making restitution to you, O gods, my lords, with reparation and a propitiatory gift on behalf of the land.

§8 (rev. 21'–40') Because you, O gods, my lords, [have] taken vengeance for the blood of Tudhaliya, those who killed Tudhaliya [have made] restitution for the blood. But this bloodshed is finished in Hatti again: Hatti too has already made restitution for it. Since it has now come upon me as well, I will also make restitution for it from my household, with restitution and a propitiatory gift. So may the soul of the gods, my lords, again be appeased. May the gods, my lords, again be well disposed toward me, and let me elicit your pity. May you listen to me, to what I plead before you. I have [not] done any evil. Of those who sinned and did the evil, no one of that day is still here. They have already died off. But because the affair of my father has come upon me, I am giving you, O gods, my lords, a propitiatory gift on account of the plague of the land, and I am making restitution. I am making restitution to you with a propitiatory gift and reparation. May you gods, my lords, again [have] mercy on me, and let me elicit your pity. Because Hatti has been oppressed by the plague, it has been reduced in size. [And those makers of offering bread and libation pourers who used to prepare] the offering bread and the libation for the gods, my lords, [since Hatti] has been severely oppressed by [the plague], [they have died] from the plague. [The plague] does not subside at all, and they continue to die, [even those] few [makers of offering bread] and libation pourers [who still remain will die, and nobody will prepare] for you offering bread and libation any longer.

§9 (rev. 41'–51') May [you gods, my lords], have mercy on [me again] because of the offering bread and the libation which [they prepare for you], and let me elicit your pity. Send the plague [away from Hatti]. Let those few makers of offering bread [and pourers of libation] who [still remain] with you not be harmed, and let them not go on dying. Let them prepare [the offering bread] and the libation for you. O gods, my lords, turn the plague [away, and send] whatever is evil to the enemy land. Whatever has happened in Hatti because of Tudhaliya, send it [away] O gods, [my lords]. Send [it] to the enemy land. May you again have mercy on Hatti, and let [the plague] subside. Furthermore, [because] I, your priest, your servant, elicit your pity, may you have mercy on me. Send away the worry from my heart, take away the anguish from my soul!

Colophon

(rev. 52'-53') [One tablet], complete. When Mursili made a plea [because of the plague . . .].

No. 13
Mursili's "Fourth" Plague Prayer
to the Assembly of Gods (arranged by localities)
(CTH 378.IV)

This plea represents the fully developed category of prayers addressed to the Assembly of gods (Houwink ten Cate 1987; Singer 1996: 153f.). The list opens with the Noble Storm-god,[15] and is followed by some thirty local deities including Iyarri, the god of war and pestilence (the Mesopotamian Erra). According to this prayer, Hatti's troubles started in the reign of Mursili's grandfather, Tudhaliya II (§4), as is indeed reported in a well-known historical retrospective (Bryce 1998: 158). Then came a period of success and growth, which was again followed by disaster caused by the war against Egypt (§5). Mursili's main concern here is the restitution of neglected temples, and he repeatedly attempts to find out through oracles by what means these reparations should be covered. The text came down to us in two double-column copies.

§1 (i 1–16) O gods, my lords: Noble Storm-god, the two lords of Landa, Iyarri, gods of Hatti, gods of Arinna, gods of Zippalanda, gods of Tuwanuwa, gods of Hupisna, gods of Durmitta, gods of Ankuwa, gods of Samuha, gods of Sarissa, gods of Hurma, gods of Hanhana, gods of Karahna, gods of Illaya, Kamrusepa of Taniwanda, gods of Zarruwisa, Storm-god of Lihzina, Protective-god of the Army Camp of His Majesty's father which is in Marassantiya, Uliliyassi of Parmanna, gods of Kattila, Storm-god of Hasuna, gods of Muwani, gods of Zazzisa, the Telipinu-gods [whose] temples in the land have been destroyed, gods of Salpa, Storm-god of Ar[ziya (?)].

§2 (i 17–20) O gods, my lords! I, Mursili, [your servant], your priest, herewith bow down to you. Lend me your ear and hear me in the matter in which I have bowed down to you.

§3 (i 21–35) O gods, my lords! Since ages past you have been inclined towards [men] and have [not] abandoned mankind. And mankind [became] populous and your divine servants [were] numerous. They always set up for the gods, [my] lords, offering bread and libation. O gods, my lords, you have turned your back on mankind. All of a sudden, in the time of my grandfather Hatti was oppressed, [and it] became [devastated] by the enemy. Mankind was [reduced in number] by plague, and your [servants] were reduced in number. And among you, [gods], my lords, [one had no] temple, and [the temple] of another [fell into ruin]. Whoever [served] before a god perished, and [your] rites [were neglected]. [No] one performed [them] for you.

§4 (i 36–46) [But] when my [father] became king, [you], O gods, my lords, stood behind him. He resettled the [depopulated] lands. [And for you], O gods, my lords, in whatever temple there were no [objects], or whatever image of god had been destroyed, my father restored what he could, though what he could not, he did not restore. O gods, my lords, you never before oppressed my father, and you never before oppressed me. But now you have oppressed me.

§5 (i 47–55) When my father went to Egyptian territory, since that day of Egypt, death has persisted in [Hatti], and from that time Hatti has been dying. My father repeatedly inquired through the oracles, but he did not find you, O gods, my lords, through the oracles. I have also repeatedly inquired of you through oracle, but I have not found you, O gods, my lords, through oracle.

§6 *In this section the scribe (of manuscript A) left an empty space of about six lines, indicating through the single word "destroyed" that the corresponding passage in the manuscript from which he was copying was damaged.*

§7 (ii 1–3) *Only a few words are preserved from this paragraph (in both copies). It probably dealt with the rites (ḫazziwita) that Mursili intended to restore.*

§8 (B ii 3'–16') *The first three lines are very fragmentary.* For whatever [god] there is [a temple], but he has no [objects], I will restore [them for him]. And for whatever god [there is no temple], I will build a temple for him. And whichever [gods] have been destroyed, I will restore for them a statue [. . . and] its [. . .] as before. *The rest of col. ii and all of col. iii, except the beginnings of lines, are lost.*

§9' (A iv 1–5) Or should I have restored it for [the gods], my lords, from my land, or from my infantry and chariotry? If I should indeed reestablish the gods, since now the members of my household, land, infantry and chariotry keep dying, by what means should I reestablish you, O gods?

§10′ *As in §6, the scribe (of manuscript A) left an empty space of about ten lines, indicating that the corresponding passage in the manuscript from which he was copying was damaged.*

§11′ (iv 16–28) And it dies, by what means should I reestablish [you]? O gods, have mercy on me again because of this [reason]! Turn(!)[16] towards me! Send the plague away from the land! Let it subside in the towns where people are dying, and let the plague not return to the towns in which it has subsided! I have [said] to myself thus: "If the aforementioned word of the god is true, [and] my father [could not discover them] through an oracle, nor could I discover them [through an oracle], should the land of Hatti [inquire by oracle] and [will it discover] them through an oracle?" And I have pled my case. [. . .] *The remaining fifteen lines or so are almost entirely lost.*

No. 14
Mursili's "Fifth" Plague Prayer to the Assembly of Gods (arranged typologically) (CTH 379)

This text, despite some formal differences, is probably another plague prayer of Mursili (Houwink ten Cate 1987: 20), rather than a "purification oath" (*Reinigungseid*), as suggested by Sürenhagen (1985). As in all plague prayers of this king, Mursili makes a concerted effort to absolve himself of any misdeed that might have led to the plague. According to its colophon, the text consisted of at least two tablets, this being the first. Less than half of the obverse and nothing of the reverse is preserved, which may explain why some characteristic parts of the exculpatory prayer are missing.

The text opens with an exceptional assembly of gods arranged by types of deities (Singer 1996: 153): "all the Storm-gods," "all the Protective-gods," etc.. After a large gap, there comes a detailed account of the Egyptian affair (see Bryce 1998: 192ff.), mentioning in passing the Hittite generals Lupakki and Tarhunta-zalma (§11) and the affair of the Egyptian widow (§12–13). Of special interest is Mursili's comment that he is unaware of any additions or omissions made by his predecessors on the tablet containing the treaty with Egypt (§8; cf. no. 11, §5). He also exculpates himself from any violations of Egyptian territory, arguing that he was still a child at the time (§12; cf. no. 21, §2).

§1 (i' 1–4) [Sun-god of Heaven], Storm-god [of . . . , Sun-goddess of] Arinna, Mezzulla, [Hulla(?)/Zintuhi(?)], Storm-god of Hatti, [Storm-god of] Zippalanta;

§2 (i 5–6) [. . .], Seri, Hurri, [Storm-god *piḫaimi*(?)], all the Storm-gods;

§3 (i 7–8) [. . .], Hebat of Kummanni, all [the Hebats], Halki;

§4 (i 9–10) All [the Sarrumas(?)], [. . .], all the Hebat-Sarrumas;

§5 (i 11–15) Protective-god (LAMMA), [Protective-god of] Hatti, all the Protective-gods, Ishtar, [Ishtar of the Field of] His Majesty, Ishtar of Samuha, [all the] Ishtars, Telipinu, all the Telipinus, War-god (ZABABA), all the War-gods;

§6 (i 16–22) Sun-goddess of the Netherworld, Lelwani, Pirwa, Marduk, Iyarri, Hasammeli, Fate-goddesses, Mother-goddesses, all the male gods of the assembly(!),[17] all the female gods of the assembly(!), the place of assembly, the place in which the gods assemble for judgment.

The rest of the column, about thirty lines, is almost entirely lost. The verbal endings at the end of lines 6"–8" in col. i(!) probably belong to second person plural imperatives, which may be addressed to the "male gods (and) female gods" mentioned in l. 5."

§7' (ii' 6') [. . .] [. . . the tablet of/about] Egypt.

§8' (ii 7'–17') To this tablet I did not add any word, nor did I remove [any]. O gods, my lords, take notice! I do not know whether any of those who were kings before me added [any word] to it or removed any. I do not know anything, and I have not heard a word of it since.

§9' (ii 18'–24') I did not concern myself with those borders which were set for us by the Storm-god. Those borders that my father left me, those borders [I kept]. I did [not] desire from him [anything]. Neither [did I take anything] from his borderland.

§10' (ii 25') [. . .] this matter [. . .]. *Gap of about two lines between KBo 31.121 and KBo 31.121a, followed by three fragmentary lines.*

§11' (KUB 31.121a ii 6"–9") [. . . infantry and] chariotry of Hatti [. . .]. [. . .] He (i.e. Suppiluliuma) sent out Lupakki and Tarhunta-zalma, and they attacked those lands.

§12' (ii 10"–15") The king of Egypt died in those very [days]. I was still a child, so I did not know whether the king of Egypt lodged [a protest(?)]

to my father about those lands, or whether he [did] nothing.

§13' (ii 16"–20") And since the wife of the king of Egypt was a widow, she wrote to my father.[. . .] to talk with women [. . .]. I, in those [. . .] I was not seen(?) [. . .]. *Some eight lines missing at the end of col. ii. All of the reverse is broken off. From the colophon on the edge of KUB 48.111 only "not complete" is preserved.*

Notes

1. For a definition of the political status of the *kuriwana*-lands, see refs. and bibliography cited in *HEG* 4: 647–649; see also Lebrun 1980: 175f.

2. Probably nothing is missing here (cf. §3), although the parallel prayer to Telipinu (no. 9, §2) adds here "the queen, your maid-servant," and in §8 "the queen your maid-servant, and the princes, your servants."

3. This translation differs somewhat from the more common rendering: "Among the deities you alone, DN, are honored" (Gurney 1940: 23; Güterbock 1980: 43, but cf. 1978: 135; *CHD* L–N: 364b). I have avoided the restrictive "alone" and "only" (for the emphatic -*pat*) in some of the following expressions as well, preferring a less-burdened comparative rendering.

4. So with Catsanicos 1991: 3 n. 5, taking the possessive pronoun of *hattatar= summit* as a clear first-person plural, rather than a second-person plural, as found in most translations (Gurney 1940: 27; Archi 1978: 83; Carruba 1983: 5; Lebrun 1980: 169; Beckman 1986: 28; Ünal 1991: 805; *HED* vol. 4: 261). This also provides a much better sense: since nothing seems to be working for them anymore, people have lost confidence in their own wisdom, rather than in the wisdom of the gods.

5. An implement with some religious meaning (Gurney 1940: 90ff.; Košak 1982: 47; Beckman 1983a: 26). Kühne 1978: 174 translates: "We will hang the bronze clasp(?) from the *sarpa* wood," and tentatively suggests that *sarpa* may be "a pendulum oracle." Ünal 1991: 806 thinks of a comb-like spatula with teeth, which would have served metaphorically to scrape away the plague ("wir es mit dem Kratzer der Spange putzen können"). Taracha 1999 also thinks of some thorny or pointed object or plant. *CHD* Š suggests "we will *kunk*-" the pins from the *sarpa*-," in the sense of "we will correct the situation." The exact significance of this idiom, which recurs in no. 10, §11 remains unknown.

6. The Middle Hittite version has (no. 7, obv. 16'f.): "the land of the Hurrian, Kuzzuwatna, and Arzawa."

7. The Middle Hittite version adds here (no. 7, obv. 19') "they constantly seek to damage Hatti."

8. The Middle Hittite version (no. 7, rev. 9) has here "You are degrading your own name," either with an omission of "do not" (Carruba 1983: 6), or rather as a bold statement about the consequences of the deity's failure to protect Hatti against her enemies (Hoffner 1977: 154, n. 16).

9. This "separate tablet of the invocation" could in fact be duplicate E, below (Carruba 1983: 9).

10. From §7 onward the numbering by paragraphs is one figure lower than in the edition of Goetze 1930.

11. An almost identical expression recurs in no. 19, §71. For the rendering of *taptappa-* as "cage" (rather than "nest"), see Singer 1996: 66.

12. That is, "they shall regularly induce dream-revelations by sleeping in the sanctuaries." See Hoffner 1987.

13. This idiomatic expression recurs in no. 8, §7; see there.

14. The missing last group of dignitaries who swore allegiance to Tudhiliya the Younger must be some lower echelon officers—"corporals," "subalterns," or the like (Beal 1992: 476, 509ff.; Beckman 1997a: 156). A restoration "servants" (Lebrun 1980: 15; Ünal 1991: 809) does not make much sense in this context.

15. The "Noble (*MULTARIHU*) Storm-god" may well be identical with the "Valiant (*muwatalli*) Storm-god," Mursili's personal deity (Goetze 1930: 250).

16. The text actually has "burn me," which makes no sense. Goetze 1930: 248 (followed by Beckman 1997a: 160) suggested an emendation of two signs to get (an unattested) form of the verb *wars-* "to appease, calm." I prefer a slight phonetic change, from *warnu-,* to *wahnu-,* "turn," which also provides an expression more common in these prayers. See also Lebrun 1980: 227, 229.

17. With a slight graphical emendation (*tuliyas* instead of *liliyas*). See *CHD* L–N: 60b; Sürenhagen 1985: 8; Houwink ten Cate 1987: 20.

IV

Mursili's Prayers Concerning His Wife and His Stepmother

With the conquest of Mittanni Suppiluliuma I joined the international scene of the ancient Near East, and according to the age-old custom of royal marriages between peer kingdoms he took the daughter of the king of Babylon as his second wife (Carruba 1998, with bibliography). Her original name still escapes us, but in Hatti she assumed the name Tawannanna, a title born by Hittite queens. She seems to have played an important role not only in the religious life of the kingdom, but also in political affairs, as shown for example by the appearance of her name alongside that of her husband on political documents from Ugarit (Otten 1975). After Suppiluliuma's death she maintained, according to Hittite tradition, her queenly rank, and she became increasingly domineering in her management of the royal household during the short reign of Arnuwanda II and the beginning of Mursili II's reign. According to the latter's testimony, her stepsons did not curtail her authority despite her abuses of power. Only when Mursili's wife, Gassul(iy)awiya, was struck down by a mysterious illness, and prayers to the gods (nos. 15–16) remained unanswered, did he begin to suspect Tawannanna's machinations behind the matter and consulted the gods through oracles (Archi 1980; Hoffner 1983). But all his efforts were to no avail, and his beloved wife died, probably in his ninth year of rule (Bryce 1998: 227, n. 70). In his grief he turned against his stepmother and banished her from the palace, depriving her of her most important religious tasks. Nevertheless, he did not take full revenge on her, even though the oracle sanctioned her execution (no. 18, §1; Hoffner 1983). Even so, he was concerned that the gods might ultimately disapprove of the deposition of their chief priestess, and this fear still haunted Mursili's son, Hattusili, who several decades later insisted in his prayer that he was still a child when all this happened (no. 21, §2). To justify his deeds, Mursili composed two highly emotional exculpatory prayers. In the first (no. 17) he seeks mainly to incriminate Tawannanna with several grave offences against the gods and against the king's family (de Martino 1998). In the second (no. 18) Mursili explains that he had divine (oracular) authority to take even more drastic measures than he did (Hoffner 1983) and he vividly contrasts his stepmother's present condition, alive, seeing the sun above and lacking nothing, to that of his deceased wife whom she had killed. He also describes in moving words his daily agony of bereavement. The four texts included under this heading contain not only fascinating historical data on Mursili's reign, but also some of the most touching personal testimonies in Hittite literature. All along, however, we must remember that we only have Mursili's account of the events and not even a shred of his "devilish" stepmother's version.

No. 15
Mursili's Prayer to Lelwani
for the Recovery of Gassuliyawiya
(CTH 380)

This substitute ritual and prayer for the recovery of Gassuliyawiya is addressed to Lelwani, an old Hattian deity (addressed here as "my lord") who became identified with the Mesopotamian Queen of the Underworld, Ereshkigal /Allatum (Otten 1950; Laroche 1974: 184f.; Hoffner 1985; Haas 1994: 420ff.). It closely resembles the ritual for the installation of a substitute king (Kümmel 1967; Gurney 1977a: 56ff.; Kühne 1978: 174ff.; Haas 1994: 207ff.). A good-looking woman was dispatched to the deity with animal and food offerings to serve as a substitute (*tarpalli* or *tarpassa*) for the mortally ill Gassuliyawiya, who is also designated here Great Daughter, a title whose exact definition is still controversial (Singer 1991; Klinger 1996: 215, n. 349; Houwink ten Cate 1996: 47ff.). The actual fate of the female substitute is not indicated. In any case, the ritual did not achieve its purpose in diverting divine wrath from the threatened victim. The identity of Gassuliyawiya in this text has been disputed, but most scholars consider her to be Mursili II's wife, rather than the daughter of Hattusili and Puduhepa who married Bentesina of Amurru (see refs. cited in Klinger 1996: 215, nn. 349–350 and Bryce 1998: 227, n. 69). If so, the person interceding on her behalf could be either Mursili himself, or, less likely, her ardent adversary, Queen Tawannanna (Dinçol et al. 1993: 98). There are three small fragments which may perhaps belong to this text (Otten 1984: 229, n. 3).

The beginning of the text is lost.
§1 (obv. 2'–9') [. . .] of the deity [. . .] now for you [. . .] one fattened cow and one [fattened] ewe [. . .] and [let] them [. . .] before the god [. . .] that anger [. . .] and the anger[1] concerning the Great Daughter [. . .]. And you, O god, eat the fat of that [fattened cow and fattened ewe] and satisfy your hunger! [Drink] the blood [and quench your thirst]!

§2 (obv. 10'–20') If you, O god, my lord, are seeking some evil in my [wife(?)], I herewith send you [my/an] adorned substitute. Compared to me she is excellent: she is pure, she is radiant, she is pale, she is endowed with everything. Examine her, O god, my lord! Let this female go back and forth before the god, my lord, and may you turn again in favor toward the Great Daughter and save her from this sickness! Remove from her this sickness and let her recover! And then it will come to pass that in the future the Great Daughter will constantly praise you, O god, and she will constantly invoke only your name, O god.

§3 (obv. 21'–31') Since Gassuliyawiya, your maid, saw you, O Lelwani, in her dream in Samuha, didn't she, your maid, make any sacrifices in those days for you, O god? But now your maid, Gassuliyawiya, has fallen ill, and sickness has oppressed her. Furthermore, that matter burdened her and they inquired about it to the gods through an oracle, and it was established by the gods too. And now Gassulawiya, your maid, because of her sickness has sent to you, O god, her substitutes: [one fattened cow,] and one fattened ewe, dressed up in festive garments, [. . .] which have been determined for the person [of Gassuliyawiya].

The rest of the obverse and the first lines of the reverse are almost entirely lost.
§4' (rev. 7'–17') [. . .] You, O Lelwani, eat the fat of [the fat cow], of the ewe and the nanny-goat [and satisfy your hunger. Drink(!) that [blood] and quench your thirst! The fat [. . .] of the fattened cow, and that of the ewe and the nanny-goat, [. . .]. Behold, Gassulawiya, your maid, [has] herewith [sent] to you this woman, O god. She has dressed [her] up in festive garments and sent you her [substitute]. If you, O god, have counted something against her, let this woman stand for you in her place. O god, my lord, remove the sickness from Gassuliyawiya!

§5' (rev. 18'–26') Furthermore, Gassulawiya, your maid, has sent to you in good will a nanny-goat(!), together with the fattened cow, the fattened ewe, bread and wine-beer. Accept, O god, this offering in good spirit and turn again in favor to Gassuliyawiya. Save her from this sickness! Take it away from her and let her recover! Then it will come to pass that in the future Gassuliyawiya will constantly praise you, O god, and she will constantly invoke [only] your name, O god. *End of the tablet.*

No. 16
Mursili's Prayer to the Sun-goddess of Arinna for the Recovery of Gassuliyawiya
(CTH 376.F)

This prayer begins with a hymn to the Sun-goddess of Arinna, which is similar to (but more concise than) the one contained in one of Mursili's plague prayers (no. 8, §§1–2). The reverse is too fragmentary for a coherent translation, but it no doubt contains a supplication for the recovery of Gassuliyawiya (ll. 8', 10'). It also mentions "the queen" (ll. 7', 9', 11'), which must refer to Tawannanna (Güterbock 1958: 244; 1978a: 137).

§1 (i? 1'–5') [I am herewith invoking you by means of offering bread and libation. So be] pacified [. . .]. [Lend] me [your ear], O Sun-goddess of Arinna, and listen to what I say to you!

§2 (i? 6'–20') [You, O Sun-goddess of Arinna, are] an honored goddess. [To you,] my [goddess, there are temples] only in Hatti, but in no other land [is there anything for you]. They provide for holy and pure festivals and rituals for you [only in Hatti], but in no other land. Lofty [temples adorned] with silver [and gold you have only in Hatti, but in no other land. There are [cups] and rhyta of silver, gold, and precious stones [only in Hatti]. They celebrate festivals for you, of the new [year], of autumn, of spring, and of the sacrificial rituals only in Hatti, [but in] no other [land.

The rest is broken. From col. ii and from the rev. only a few beginnings of lines are left.

No. 17
Mursili's Accusations against Tawannanna
(CTH 70)

Since his pleas to Lelwani (no. 15) and to the Sun-goddess of Arinna (no. 16) have evidently failed to cure his ailing wife, Mursili became convinced that the real reason for Gassuliyawiya's grave illness were the curses of Tawannanna, which may be referred to in late oracular inquiries as well (van den Hout 1998: 42). She repeatedly asked the gods to punish Mursili's family for sins that, according to Mursili, she herself committed. Eventually she succeeded in bringing about Gassuliyawiya's death (§§4', 6'). At this point Mursili turned to the gods, accusing his stepmother not only of killing his wife, but also of a series of serious abuses of power which justifed her banishment from the palace and the curtailment of her excessive power.

The preserved part of this exculpatory prayer begins with Mursili's statement that when he assumed kingship he had not interfered in any way with Tawannanna's authority, even though some of her activities were "not right" (§2). He then proceeds (§3') to expose her depletion of the material resources of the royal palace in order to enrich her own protégés, who apparently had their power base in the Stone House, a cultic institution which probably served as a royal mausoleum. Much speculation has revolved around the nature of the "things" she brought with her from Babylonia and distributed among the population of Hatti. The more tantalizing options, from sorcery to prostitution, must probably be given up in favor of the more prosaic possibility that her own dowry is referred to, which she spent entirely in the pursuit of enhancing her popularity in Hatti and winning over influential supporters for her devious concoctions (Imparati 1977: 37, n. 60; de Martino 1998: 41ff.). In the next section (§4') Mursili exculpates his deceased wife of slanders of conspiracy with the maidservant Annella, and accuses the queen of sending the conjurer Mezzulla to curse his wife to death.

The next paragraphs cover developments in the Tawannanna affair which occurred outside the capital. Reference is made here to events which are also recorded in Mursili's annals and in other texts, and can thus be dated with some accuracy. In his ninth year the king celebrated in Kummanni a festival of Hebat (Goetze 1933: 109; Trémouille 1997: 107–110), and used this opportunity to beg the goddess for the well-being of his family (§5'). He also summoned to Kummanni his ill brother Sharre-Kushuh, king of Karkamish, who died shortly afterwards. He must be the "sick man" referred to in the next fragmentary passage (§6'), who was interrogated on his sick-bed by Tawannanna, or one of her agents, with regard to the affair of the missing silver of the land of Ashtata. Tawannanna, who must have had access to the treasuries of state temples, is quoted as exonerating herself before the goddess Ishara for the disappearance of the silver, and blaming it on Gassuliyawiya instead. We shall probably never know what actually happened to the missing treasure. The last fragmentary section (§7') refers to Mursili's campaign to the land of Azzi/Hayasa in his tenth year (Goetze 1933: 131ff.; van den Hout 1998: 42–44). Of outstanding chronological importance is the report on the sun omen, which from the earliest days of Hittitology has been interpreted as a solar eclipse (Forrer 1926: 3f.). Although many have doubted the validity of this interpretation, recent studies on Near Eastern chronology have validated the plausibility of its referring to an eclipse in either 1312 or 1308 B.C.E. (Houwink ten Cate 1987: 32, n. 50; Wilhelm and Boese 1987: 105ff.). The sun omen in Azzi was apparently interpreted by Tawannanna in real Babylonian fashion, as predicting the king's imminent death, and she may have schemed to install her own son on the throne of Hatti.[2]

Clearly, the long list of Tawannanna's abuses, with the alleged killing of the king's wife at the top, is emphatically described to the gods by the mourning Mursili as a preparatory step for the banishment of his stepmother from the palace and the curtailment of her cultic functions as chief priestess, as described in the next expiatory prayer (no. 18).

§1 (i 1'–4') Beginning lost. [. . .] did [not] harm her in any way. [. . .] was exposed. Subsequently my brother [. . .] her. But my father harmed her in no way.

§2 (i 5'–17') [When my father] died (lit. became god), Arnuwanda, [my brother, and I] did not harm Tawannanna at all, nor did we curtail her power [in any way]. As [she had governed the palace] and the land of Hatti during the reign of my father, in that same way she governed them [during the reign of my brother.] And when my brother [died (lit. became god), I also did not harm] Tawannanna at all, nor did I [curtail] her [power] in any way. As she governed the palace and the land of Hatti [during the reign of my father and during the reign of] my brother, [likewise] she governed them then. The privilege [and rights(?)] that she had [at the time] of her husband, and that which was forbidden to her [at the time of her husband, I did not change at all(?)]. And the privileges and rights(?) she carried on. As with her man [she had ruled Hatti, so in the same way as a widow] she ruled Hat[ti in the same way. [. . .]

The rest of col. i and the first lines of col. ii are badly damaged.

§3' (ii 3'–iii 3) [. . .] she ruined. Do you, O gods, not see how she has turned all my father's estate over to the *hekur*-house of the Protective-god, the Stone House of the gods?[3] This she let come from Shanhara (Babylon), and that she handed over in Hatti to the entire population,[4] and she left nothing. Do you gods not see? Even then I did not say anything to her and therefore I set it aright. She shut up mouths.[5] Even that which was not yet done she gave away.[6] She destroyed my father's estate. Furthermore, she even supported evil. Day and night she stands before the gods and [curses my] wife. And when I draw back the gods with offering bread and libation, and I constantly give them sacrificial bread [and libation], I make many vows to them for myself, [my wife, my son], my house, my land, and (my) brothers. [. . .]. Tawannanna, however, stands [day and night] before [the gods and curses] my wife [before the gods . . .] she keeps libating. My wife's [. . .]. O gods, do you [. . .] an untrue [. . .]? [Will you hand my wife over] to an evil judgment?

The first lines of col. III are very fragmentary, but they seem to contain a continuation of Mursili's pleading with the gods to listen to the case of his wife.

§4' (iii 4–22)[7] When she put up Annella, [the maidservant, . . .], Annella said [to my wife as following]: "Those which [. . .] the queen [sent (?)] Mezzulla to them [. . .] and [she started] to utter conjurations [. . .]." The thing which [she revealed] to my wife, [that] thing she concealed from the queen. Did my wife reveal [it] to someone [else], or did she reveal [it] to me? Or did she make it into a lawsuit and involve [the queen] in some trial? Rather, [my wife] became an informer for the queen and [behold], she banished Annella, the maidservant, from the palace. Further, if my wife had [become] an informer for the queen, had she thereby done any harm? Why did the queen turn that matter into a sin of my wife? She stands day and night before the gods and curses my wife before the gods. [She . . .] her, and she wishes for her death saying: "Let her die!" O gods, my lords, why do you listen to this evil talk? Did my wife cause any harm to the queen? Did she curtail her power in any way? And yet, Tawannanna killed my wife.

§5' (iii 23–33) When I went to Kummanni—my father had promised a Festival of Invocation to Hebat of Kummanni, but he had not yet given it to her, so she troubled me—I went to Kizzuwatna saying as follows: "Let me fulfill the promise(?) of my father!" I constantly implored and invoked Hebat of Kummanni for myself, my wife, my son, my house, my land, and the brothers [. . .].

The rest of col. iii and the first 9 lines of col. iv are almost entirely lost.

§6' (iv 10–23) [. . .] to the king of Karkamish I said: "[You ask(?)] me for the silver of Ashtata. Well,] the queen has [it!] So quit asking!" [. . .] The queen should know. Or the matter of the silver the king of Karkamish [. . .]. If I said so, you, [O gods, should know]. Didn't I tell about the matter of the silver to the king of Karkamish? She went [. . .] and pulled out (from) the mouth of the sick man,[8] [and he said]: "His Majesty said that the queen has the silver of Ashtata." [But she] kept saying to Ishara of

Ashtata: "O Goddess, [it isn't] I who have that [silver]. The one who has your, the god's, silver, the one who continually fills [. . .], don't you, O goddess, seize him? [Don't] you seize his wife and his children? Instead, you seize me, the innocent one. Seize him, or seize his wife and his children! But don't seize me [. . .]." And the queen continually cursed me, my wife, and my son before Ishara. She continually sacrificed against us.[9] Because of this my wife died.

§7' (iv 24–37) [When] I marched to the land of Azzi, the Sun-god gave an omen. The queen [in Hatti(?)] kept saying: "This omen which the Sun-god gave, [what did it] predict? Did it not predict the king's death?[10] And if [it predicted that, will the people(?)] of Hatti [seek someone] else for lordship? Will they [join(?)] lady Amminnaya and [the son(?)] of Amminnaya?" I, My Majesty, [. . .] in the land of Hayasa [. . .] he/she responded in a tablet [. . .] he/she commanded [. . .]. But when from Hayasa [I returned(?). . .] he/she suddenly refused [. . .]. When they hear this thing [. . .] I asked: "This [thing(?)] which [. . .] he/she did not conceal [. . .] said, [. . .] said. *Broken.*

No. 18
Mursili's Exculpation
for the Deposition of Tawannanna
(CTH 71)

After the death of his beloved wife Gassuliyawiya, Mursili finally decided to turn against his stepmother, who was allegedly responsible for her death. But a new join has revealed that, contrary to previous restorations of the text, Mursili did not execute Tawannanna, although oracular consultation fully confirmed her guilt (Hoffner 1983). He only banished her from the palace, depriving her from the influential post of (high-)priestess.[11] But given the special relationship between the Hittite queen and the Sun-goddess of Arinna, Mursili feared divine punishment, and this concern is still echoed in a prayer of his son, Hattusili (no. 21, §2). His daily agony over the loss of his wife is contrasted, in dramatic words, with the comfortable life led by his ill-disposed stepmother.

The beginning of the text is lost.
§1 (ii 1'- iii 4) [. . .] she killed [my wife . . .] she bereaved(?) me [. . .] . . . [. . .]. Was it a capital crime for me if she was not executed? I consulted the gods, my lords, and it was determined for me by oracle to execute her. To dethrone her was also determined for me by oracle. But even then I

did not execute her; I only deposed her from the office of priestess. Since it was determined for me by oracle to dethrone her, I dethroned her and I gave her an estate. Nothing is lacking that she desires. She has food and drink (lit. bread and water) and everything stands at her disposal. She lacks nothing. She is alive. She sees the Sun-god of Heaven with her eyes and eats the bread of life. I imposed only this one punishment, I punished her with this one thing: I sent her down from the palace and I deposed her from the office of priestess for the gods. I imposed only this one punishment. O gods, set this case down before yourselves and investigate it! Has now her life gone bad? Because she is alive, she sees the Sun-god of Heaven with her eyes and eats the bread of life. And my punishment is the death of my wife. Has it gone any better? Because she killed her, throughout the days of my life [my soul(?)] goes down to the dark Netherworld [on her account(?)] and it . . . -s for me. She has bereaved(?) me. Don't you, O gods [recognize] who was really punished?

§2' (iii 5–27) Now because I deposed [the queen] from priesthood, I will provide for the [offerings] of the gods, [my lords], and I will regularly worship the gods. Don't install [her back] to priesthood for the gods! Don't take her into account [at all]! Because she was not [. . . -ed] for *uwashuraya* while she was queen, [therefore she kept cursing my wife] until she killed her. When I had de[posed her] from priesthood [for the gods], I demoted her. I sent [the queen] down [from] the palace, and now does she not continue to curse [your priest and your servant]? [. . .] somehow. [Since] you listened to her once before, [will you] now [. . .] the same, O gods, my lords? [Will you hear] the word of evil? I, Mursili, [the Great King, King of Hatti,] herewith come forward, [and in whatever matter] I bow down [to you . . ., lend me your ear] and hear me! *The rest of the column is very damaged.*

Notes

1. Both occurrences of "anger" in this paragraph are in accusative and therefore direct object.

2. Van den Hout 1998: 44 suggests that Amminnaya, who appears in §7' in fragmentary context, could have been the name of Mursili's Babylonian stepmother, who schemed perhaps to crown her own son in the case of Mursili's utimely death. The same name occurs in KUB 188.42, 6', a small oracle fragment, and in KUB 19.84, 7', a larger fragment which may actually belong to CTH 70 (see de Martino 1998: 20, n. 6).

3. For these cultic institutions, see Imparati 1977. It is not evident whether the reference here is to two different edifices or to different designations of the same institution, probably a rock sanctuary.

4. Güterbock in Laroche 1956: 103 (followed by Hoffner 1983: 191; de Martino 1998: 33) translates: "One thing she let come from Shanhara, another thing she gave away in Hattusa to the whole populatioin."

5. "Lit. "bound the mouths." This phrase may perhaps refer to the silencing of public opinion in Hattusa through bribery (de Martino 1998: 43). It is unlikely that it refers to Tawannanna's responsibility for Mursili's speech disturbances, as suggested by some scholars (Goetze 1957: 93; Bin-Nun 1975: 186f.).

6. The text has in fact "she gave away to you (-*ta*)," but this does not seem to fit the context.

7. The reconstruction of §§4' and 6' is hampered by the difficulty in distinguishing between affirmative sentences and rhetorical questions. Also, it is difficult to establish the exact limits of direct speech and the identity of the speaker in each quotation. The reconstruction below follows in part that of de Martino 1998, who also deals with the affair of the silver of Ashtata in combination with other sources.

8. Lit., "she drew away the mouth of the sick man." From the context it would seem that the "sick man" was the king of Karkamish, who was interrogated on his sickbed by the queen herself or by one of her informers.

9. Or "sacrificed us." The phrase must certainly have a negative sense, perhaps with an ironic tone.

10. So with Hoffner 1986: 90 (LUGAL ÚŠ) and de Martino 1998: 30f., n. 90; but cf. van den Hout 1998: 43 (LUTAL-*pát*).

11. *siwanzanni*, literally "mother-of-god," is the standard designation for Hittite priestesses, usually not of very high position (Bin Nun 1975: 191ff.). Though this is not explicitly stated, Tawannanna must have acted as the chief of all the "mothers-of-god," a position which assured for her considerable powers of allocating votive offerings and perhaps even temple lands (Hoffner 1983: 191).

V

Muwatalli's Prayers

Although the reign of Muwatalli II, the great victor of the Battle of Qadesh, was one of the most eventful periods in Hittite history, the number of texts safely attributed to him is quite limited. The reason is obvious: the transfer of the Hittite capital from Hattusa to Tarhuntassa, where probably most of his texts still await discovery. The common view which explains Muwatalli's drastic move in terms of military strategy—the threat of the Kaska tribes and proximity to the Egyptian front—is in serious need of revision (Singer 1996: 191ff.; 1998; cf. Klengel 1999a: 210). Rather, the building of a new capital in southern Anatolia was part of a premeditated religious reform, replacing the traditional northern focus of Hittite cult with a strong southern orientation. This tendency is clearly reflected in Muwatalli's prayers, which exhibit a strong Hurro-Luwian influence, both in cultic terminology and in the choice of invoked deities. The prolonged neglect of southern cults, which has obviously raised the anger of the gods, is the connecting thread running along these prayers. This motif is most clearly expressed in the penitential prayer no. 19, which focuses on the important cult center of Kummanni in Kizzuwatna. No. 20 is addressed to all the gods of the lands, but there is a marked switch in focus towards the peripheral regions in the south, where the new capital was about to be established. Another fragmentary list of local gods (KBo 9.98+) strongly resembles in structure the long list in no. 20, but it adds a separate entry for the gods of Tarhuntassa. It could belong to a third prayer of Muwatalli, which was already composed after the transfer of the capital (Singer 1996: 165ff.). The theological innovations introduced by Muwatalli, which are characterized, among other things, by prayers addressed only to male gods and intercessors

(Storm-god, Sun-god, Seri), are apparently superseded after his death, when the cultic focus is redirected towards the great goddesses (Sun-goddess of Arinna, Hebat of Kummanni, and Ishtar/Sausga of Samuha) and their children (Storm-god of Nerik/Zippalanda, Mezzulla, Sarruma).

In style, the prayers of Muwatalli are characterized by a clear layout and an idiosyncratic spirit of meticulous precision striving to cover all theoretical possibilities. Some of the imagery is already found in the prayers of his father (e.g. the bird in the cage maxim, no. 11, §9 = no. 20, §71), and the short intercession to the Sun-god of Heaven (no. 20, §§66–68) has much in common with other prayers to solar deities. But on the whole, Muwatalli's prayers exhibit considerable originality and imagination.

No. 19
Muwatalli's Prayer to the Storm-god
Concerning the Cult of Kummanni
(CTH 382)

This typical plea of confession and penitence to the Storm-god was dictated, according to its colophon, by the king himself. Since the text deals with the cult of Kummanni (classical Comana Cappadociae), and the gods mentioned in it (Hebat, Sarruma, Huzzi, Hutanni) were venerated in the southern province of Kizzuwatna, it has generally been assumed that the the conjured deity is the Storm-god of Kummanni (Houwink ten Cate/Josephson 1967; Lebrun 1980: 294). However, his epithets "Lord of Heaven and Earth" and "King of gods" may point to a more universal hypostasis of the Storm-god, perhaps even to the Storm-god of Lightning (*pihassassi*), Muwatalli's personal deity, who also had Kizzuwatnean origins (Singer 1996: 162, 185ff.). The systematic search for possible reasons for the Storm-god's anger includes disputes between him and local deities (§§2–3), human transgression against local gods and holy places (§§4–7), violation of codes of social justice (§10'), desecration of holy entities (§11'), expropriation of divine property (§12'), and inadmissible speech (§13'). If it is a matter of human transgression, the king takes the responsibility for placating the angry god, but if the Storm-god's anger has been caused by some local deity, it is the Netherworld deities (*Annunaki*) who are invoked to reconcile between the discordant parties. To be noted is the usage of the first person plural throughout the text, typical of rituals with Hurrian influence (de Roos 1998) . Does it refer to the king and the queen, or rather to the king and his people? Also noteworthy is the reference to the primordial order in §1: the sky, the earth, and the sun that stood witness when the sin was committed still keep their place now to witness the expiation of that sin by Muwatalli, and are therefore invoked to dispel the Storm-god's wrath.

The occasion for the prayer seems to be a general decline in the state of the land of Kizzuwatna/Kummanni, perhaps caused by a period of drought (§12).[1] Its cause, as conceived by Muwatalli, was a prolonged neglect of its cults and even an abuse of its riches that occurred in the days of his father (§12'). In his parental criticism Muwatalli follows the tradition established by his own father, Mursili II, who blamed the plague in Hatti on Suppiluliuma I (nos. 12–16). Muwatalli solemnly vows to renew the cult provisions in this important province, matching past conditions, as learned from written records and old men or through divinatory means (§§4, 7). Like his father Mursili (no. 8, §10), he protests against collective punishment of the whole land, and asks for a restrictive penalty for the culpable town or house only (§§6, 10).

Invocation of gods

§1 (obv. 1–13) We have invoked the Storm-god, lord of heaven and earth, king of the gods, and [we confess] offence and sin before him, [and we dispel the Storm-god's anger]. We have invoked Hebat, queen of heaven, and we dispel the Storm-god's anger. [We have invoked Sarruma(?) . . .], and we dispel the Storm-god's anger. We have invoked the gods of the lands, mountains, rivers, [sources and springs, and we dispel the Storm-god's anger]. We have invoked Huzzi and Hutanni, and [we dispel] the Storm-god's anger. [We have invoked the Sun-god of Heaven(?)], and we dispel the Storm-god's anger. We have invoked Heaven and Earth. The heaven [that was standing above . . .] then, that same heaven is still standing above now. The earth that [was lying] below then, [that same earth is still lying below now.] The Sun-god of Heaven who then stood in the sky above, that same [Sun-god of Heaven is still standing in the sky above] now. And he stands to witness the dispelling of the Storm-god's wrath. We have invoked [. . .], and we dispel the Storm-god's anger. [May] the gods [tell(?)] the gods [. . .]. May the soul of the god be conciliatory toward the population and the land, and [may the Storm-god(?). . .] regard [us(?)] now with conciliatory eyes. I, My Majesty, Muwatalli, lord of the lands, [have] just invoked] them, [and I make this plea]. May the Storm-god, my lord, listen to it. May the Storm-god, my lord, hear how I dispel the sins of the lands and make [that into] this plea.

Penitence for Sins and Imploration
for the Resumption of Favorable Conditions

§2 (obv. 14–15) If some god of the land has angered the Storm-god, may the Netherworld deities (*Anunnaki*) now reconcile the Storm-god to that deity. May the Storm-god regard the land with conciliatory eyes again, and may wealth, peace, well-being, growth, prosperity and maturation(?)[2] [come about] in the land.

§3 (obv. 16–17) If mountains, rivers, wells or springs have angered the Storm-god in some way, may the Netherworld deities now reconcile the Storm-god with (those) mountains, rivers, wells [or springs]. May the Storm-god, my lord, regard the land with conciliatory eyes again, and may the same things (i.e. the above-mentioned list) come about in the land.

§4 (obv. 18–28) If some god of the land is offended and has pleaded with the Storm-god, [now I, My Majesty], Muwatalli, [lord of the lands,] make that into a plea, and may the Storm-god, my lord, listen to it(!).[3] The land was great, but it has receded. [. . .]. But when I, My Majesty, solicit the gods to the Land of Kummanni [. . .], [what(?)] does not fulfill the requirements of the gods, [I will ask(?)] the people who are still there and who were there with my father and [my grandfather(?)]. And whatever I, My Majesty, discover now in the written records,[4] I will carry out. [But whatever] requirements [of the gods] I do not manage to fulfill, that] you know, O Storm-god, my lord. When I consult a venerable old man, [as] they remember [each(?)] requirement and report it, thus I shall carry it out. And now, while I resettle the land and you open up(?) to the population, in the fallow land wine and fertility will result.[5] And while the land returns to its former state, the gods of the land will regain their position just as they were before. While I am resettling the land, and until it recovers(?), I shall indeed perform the protocol of the gods which I am rediscovering, and it shall be henceforth carried out. May the Storm-god, my lord, speak to the gods, and let the gods regard the land with conciliatory eyes, and let them bring about wealth, maturation(?), peace, well-being, and growth in the land.

§5 (obv. 29–31) If mountains, rivers, sources, springs and fountains of the land keep the Storm-god, my lord, angry, may the Netherworld deities now reconcile the Storm-god with the mountains, rivers, sources and springs. May the Storm-god, my lord, regard the land with conciliatory eyes again, and may wealth, peace and growth come about in the land.

§6 (obv. 32–39) If some mountain, or a *sinapsi*-sanctuary,[6] some holy place, has been offended and has pleaded with the Storm-god, [I, My Majesty, Muwatalli, herewith] shall set it right again now. Those towns that are inhabited and have a *sinapsi*-sanctuary, they shall be surveyed and [shall be set right]. In accordance with the consecration (rites), they shall be reconsecrated precisely. And if something has been corrupted, as soon as it is known, it shall be reconsecrated precisely. If there are any *sinapsi*-sanctuaries in any of the deserted towns, [as they used to celebrate(?)] them, so precisely shall they begin to celebrate them. If some single town, or some single house does wrong, take vengeance for it, O god, on that single town, or on that single house, and [destroy] it. But do not take vengeance for it on the land. May the Storm-god, my lord, [regard] the land with conciliatory eyes [again].

§7 (obv. 40–44) If someone has overturned the throne of the Storm-god, or a stela (*huwasi*), or if he has blocked a sacred spring, [. . .], I will set it right again. But what I do not find or discover in a written record, [or] what a venerable old man does not report to me, clarify this matter to me, O god, in a dream. [I, My Majesty, Muwatalli(?), herewith] shall set it right fully and shall carry out the order of the god. May the Storm-god, my lord, [regard the land with conciliatory eyes again], and may [wealth], peace, well-being, maturation(?) and growth come about in the land.

§8 (obv. 45–48) [. . .] in evil curse, blood, tears, [. . .]. Behold now, in this [. . .

The rest of the paragraph is almost entirely broken away. Almost half of the reverse is missing.

§9' (rev. 1'–2') *Only traces left.*

§10' (rev. 3'–8') If some people give orphans [. . .], and he has pleaded with Sarruma, and Sarruma [has pleaded] with the Storm-god [. . .], they shall set it right again. And that which is lost, [. . .] there also they shall set it right. Even if it is [the house] of a poor man, take vengeance for it, O Storm-god, my lord, on that house [. . .]. But do not [take vengeance] for it on the land.

§11' (rev. 9'–11') If <they . . .-ed> from an evil bird by(?) an augur,[7] or if someone [defiled(?)] the bread of a dead person, behold, they have now treated that bird and they have released it. And these [. . .]. They have purified the bread of the dead person.

§12' (rev. 12'–23') If he has given away these good things of the Land of Kummanni, and if the god(?) [has demanded(?)] them, and if he appealed to the deity of Arusna, now behold, in that matter the king's father [is responsible].[8] Take vengeance [on him]! And they perform the *arawanna*-ritual of the deity of Arusna, and [. . .] them. Since we are only human, the words which we know, [which came] forth from our mouths, [. . .], and those which we do not know, which did not come forth from our mouths, [if] they [are the cause of anger(?)], may the Netherworld deities look for them in the dark earth. [May they find them(?) . . .] that day, and may they be dispelled. May the Storm-god, my lord, [regard] the land of Kummanni with conciliatory eyes. Just as the Storm-god fills the mother's breast for our benefit, [so let . . .]. And just as we are satisfied with cold water, in this same way [let] the Stormgod, my lord, [give us(?)] water(?) [. . .]. May it be saturation for mankind, but for the Storm-god, my lord, [let it be] a matter of praise. Sacrificial bread will become plentiful in the land, and wine offering [. . .]. [may] the Storm-god, my lord, [favour(?)/listen to(?)] the good people!

Colophon

(rev. 24'–27') One tablet of the presentation of the plea to the Storm-god, written down [from the mouth(?)] of His Majesty. Complete. Written by the hand of Lurma(-ziti),[9] junior incantation priest, apprentice [of . . .], son of Aki-Tessub.

No. 20
Muwatalli's Model Prayer to the Assembly of Gods through the Storm-god of Lightning
(CTH 381)

This plea of Muwatalli is the longest and best preserved Hittite prayer (290 lines). Its redactional history is reflected in the script of the two main contemporary exemplars: an original version (B), written from dictation, was copied, with corrections, by a second scribe (A), and both versions were "proofread" by an instructor, who also introduced a "postscript" (§93) in text A (Houwink ten Cate 1968; Singer 1996: 135ff.).

This prayer has an idiosyncratic and perfectly lucid structure. The preamble (cf. no. 5) is exceptional in its edict-like formulation (Houwink ten Cate 1987: 30, n. 35). It is followed by a rare description of the ritual preparations performed on the roof (§1). The invoked deities comprise the totality of the assembly of gods, divided into two distinct groups: "the gods of Hatti" (§2) and "the gods of the lands" (§§6–65), a theological-geographical concept which covers the central districts of the Hittite kingdom (Singer 1994; 1996: 175ff.). The latter group contains the largest number of deities listed within a single Hittite text: 140 deities belonging to 83 different localities. The offerings are divided accordingly between the two groups (§§75–87 and 89–92, respectively), and are eventually burnt on the roof (§93). Each general invocation of gods is preceded by the invocation of intercessory gods, who are asked to convene the assembly and to guarantee a successful audience for the suppliant. The gods of Hatti are approached by the sacred bull Seri, the champion of Hatti (§5); the gods of the lands are approached first by the Sun-god of Heaven (§66–68), and then by the Storm-god of Lightning, Muwatalli's personal god (§69–74). This last intercession is in itself a self-contained prayer formulated in hymnic style. Curiously, the prayer is lacking any confessions of actual sins and also any specific request of the suppliant. It simply serves as an all-purpose model prayer, the actual causes to be inserted whenever the occasion arises (§88). The translation below follows text A, noting significant variants in B.

Preamble and Preparations for the Ritual Offerings

§1 (i 1–9) Thus says *tabarna* Muwatalli, Great King, king of Hatti, son of Mursili, Great King, king of Hatti, the hero: If some problem burdens a man('s conscience), he makes a plea to the gods. He places on the roof, facing the Sun, two covered wickerwork tables: He places one table for the Sun-goddess of Arinna, and for the male gods one table. On them there are: 35 thick breads of a handful of moist flour, a thin bowl of honey mixed with fine oil, a full pot of fat-bread, a full bowl of groats, thirty pitchers of wine. And when he prepares these, the king goes up to the roof and he bows before the Sun-god of Heaven.

Invocation of the Gods of Hatti

§2 (i 10–19) He says as follows: Sun-god of Heaven and Sun-goddess of Arinna, my lady, Queen, my lady, queen of Hatti, Storm-god, king of Heaven, my lord, Hebat Queen, my lady, Storm-god of Hatti, king of Heaven, lord of Hatti, my lord, Storm-god of Ziplanda, my lord, beloved son of the Storm-god, lord of the Land of Hatti, Seri and Hurri (*B*: Seri, the bull who is champion in Hattusa, the land), all the male gods and the female gods, all the mountains and the rivers of the Land of Hatti, my lords. Divine lords—Sun-goddess of Arinna, my lady, and all the gods of the Land of Hatti, my lords—whose priest I am, who have conferred upon me, from among all others, the rulership over Hatti.

Agenda of the Pleas to Follow

§3 (i 20–24) Now, gods, listen to me, to the word and plea of me, your priest, your servant. First, I shall make a plea with regard to yourselves, my divine lords, about your temples, about your statues; how the gods of Hatti are treated and also how they are mistreated.

§4 (i 25–32) Thereafter, I shall make the matters of my own soul into a plea. Divine lords, lend me your ear, and listen to these my pleas! And the words which I will make into a plea to the divine lords, these words, divine lords, accept and listen to them! And whatever words you do not wish to hear from me, and I nevertheless persist in making them into a plea to the gods, they merely emerge from my human mouth; refrain from listening to them, divine lords.

Invocation of Seri, Herald of Hatti

§5 (i 33–36) Seri, my lord, bull of the Storm-god, champion of Hatti (lit.: the one who steps in front in the Land of Ḫatti). In these words of the presentation of the plea introduce me before the gods. Let the divine lords listen to these words and plea, the divine lords of heaven and earth (*B* adds: all of them).

Invocation of the Gods of All the Lands[10]

§6 (i 37–39) Sun-god of Heaven, Sun-goddess of Arinna, Storm-god of Arinna, Mezzulla, Hulla, Zinduhiya, male gods, female gods, mountains and rivers of Arinna, Storm-god of Salvation, Storm-god of Life.

§7 (i 40) Storm-god of Lightning, Hebat of Samuha, male gods, female gods, mountains and rivers of Samuha (*B*: Tiwa).

§8 (i 41–42) Storm-god of Lightning, Sun-goddess of Arinna, Hebat, queen of Heaven, Storm-god of the Ruin, gods of the palace of the grandfather.

§9 (i 43–45) Storm-god of Halab, Hebat of Halab, Ishtar of the Field of Samuha, Lady of the *ayakku,* Apara of Samuha, male gods, female gods, mountains and rivers of Samuha.

§10 (i 46–47) Valiant Storm-god, Hebat, Storm-god of Sahpina, male gods, female gods, mountains and rivers of Kadapa.

§11 (i 48–49) Storm-god of Help, Queen of Kadapa, male gods, female gods, mountains and rivers of Kadapa, Storm-god of Thunder, all the Storm-gods.

§12 (i 50–53) Storm-god of Hatti, Prominent Calf, Storm-god of the Army, Sun-god of Hatti, Protective-god of Hatti, Storm-god of Halab and Hebat of Halab of Hatti, Aya, Damkina, ZABABA, Halmasuit, Allatum, Ishtar of Nineveh, *lulahi*-gods, Kubaba.

§13 (i 54–56) Ishtar of Haddarina, Pirwa, Asgasipa, Mount Piskurunuwa, male gods, female gods, mountains and rivers of Hatti, Karzi, Hapandaliya, Mount Tatta, Mount Summiyara.

§14 (i 57–58) Storm-god of Ziplanda, Mount Daha, male gods, female gods, mountains and rivers of Ziplanda.

§15 (i 59–60) Zithariya, Storm-god of the Army, son of the Storm-god, Protective-god of the *kursas,* mountains and rivers of Zithara.

§16 (i 61) [. . .], Sun-goddess of Arinna, male gods, female gods, mountains and rivers of Urauna.

§17 (i 62–65) Storm-god of Kummanni, Hebat of Kummanni, Storm-god of the *sinapsi,* Hebat of the *sinapsi,* Storm-god of Mount Manuziya, Ningal, Pisanuhi, Mount Gallistapa, male gods, female gods, mountains and rivers of Kummanni and of the Land of Kummanni.

§18 (i 66–67) Storm-god *pihami,* Goddess of the Storm-god *pihami* of Sanahuita, male gods, female gods, mountains and rivers of Sanahuita.

§19 (i 68–70) Storm-god of Neriqqa, ZABABA ditto, Telipinu, Zahapuna, Mount Zaliyanu, Mount Zaliyanu of Gastama, Tazzuwasi, male gods and female gods of Gastama.

§20 (i 71–72) Protective-god of Hatenzuwa, Mount Haharwa, male gods and female gods of Neriqqa and of the Land of Takupsa.

§21 (i 73) Storm-god of Sarissa, Ishtar-*li,* male gods and female gods of Sarissa.

§22 (i 74–75) Storm-god of Hurma, Hantidassu of Hurma, Storm-god and Hebat of Halab of Hurma, male gods, female gods, mountains and rivers ditto.

§23 (i 76–77) Hasigasnawanza of Lawan(z)atiya!, Mulliyara, male gods, female gods, mountains and rivers of Lawazantiya.

§24 (i 78–79) Storm-god of [Pittiy]arik(?). \ Storm-god of Uda, Hebat-Sarruma, male gods, female gods, mountains and rivers of Uda.

§25 (ii 1–2) Deity of Parsa, Sun-goddess of the Netherworld, male gods, female gods, mountains and rivers of Parsa.

§26 (ii 3–4) Storm-god of Hissashappa, Storm-god of Kuliwisna, male gods and female gods of the palace of His Majesty.

§27 (ii 5–6) Storm-god of Garahna, Protective-god of Garahna, Alā, Storm-god of the Ruin, male gods, female gods, mountains and rivers of Karahna.

§28 (ii 7) Storm-god of Sugazziya, Zulima, male gods and female gods of Sugazziya.

§29 (ii 8–9) Storm-god of Lihsina, Tasimi, male gods, female gods, mountains and rivers of Lihsina.

§30 (ii 10–11) Telipinu of Durmitta, male gods, female gods, mountains and rivers of Durmitta.

§31 (ii 12–14) Storm-god of Nenassa, Lusiti of Nenassa, Marassantiya River, male gods, female gods, mountains and rivers of Nenassa.

§32 (ii 15–17) Huwassana (GAZ.BA.IA) of Hupisna, Storm-god of Hupisna, ZABABA of Hupisna, Mount Sarlaimi, male gods, female gods, mountains and rivers of Hupisna.

§33 (ii 18–19) Storm-god of Tuwanuwa, Sahhassara of Tuwanuwa, male gods, female gods, mountains and rivers of Tuwanuwa.

§34 (ii 20–21) Storm-god of Illaya, ZABABA of Illaya, male gods, female gods, mountains and rivers of Illaya.

§35 (ii 22–23) Suwanzipa of Suwanzana, male gods, female gods, mountains and rivers of Suwanzana.

§36 (ii 24–25) ZABABA of Arziya, male gods, female gods, mountains and rivers of Arziya.

§37 (ii 26–27) Storm-god of Hurniya, the King(ly) god of Hurniya, male gods, female gods, mountains and rivers of Hurniya.

§38 (ii 28–29) Storm-god of Zarwisa, Nawatiyala of Zarwisa, male gods, female gods, mountains and rivers of Zarwisa.

§39 (ii 30–31) Mighty Goddess of Sahhaniya, Storm-god of Sahhaniya, male gods, female gods, mountains and rivers of Sahhaniya.

§40 (ii 32–33) Storm-god of Pahtima, Storm-god of Sahhuwiya, Sun-god(dess) of Malitaskuriya.

§41 (ii 34–35) Washaliya of Harziuna, Storm-god of Harziuna, male gods, female gods, mountains and rivers of Harziuna.

§42 (ii 36–37) Zanduza of Sallapa, the Lord, Storm-god of Sallapa, male gods, female gods, mountains and rivers of Sallapa.

§43 (ii 38–40) Storm-god of Ussa, Storm-god of Parashunta, Mount Huwalanuwanda, Hulaya River, male gods, female gods, mountains and rivers of the Lower Land.

§44 (ii 41–42) Ishtar of Wasuduwanda, Hebat of Wasuduwanda, Ishtar of Innuwita.

§45 (ii 43–45) Storm-god of Alazhana, Telipinu of Hanhana, Ammama of Hanhana, Mount Takurga, male gods, female <gods>, mountains and rivers of Hahana.

§46 (ii 46–47) Telipinu of Tawiniya, Katahha, male gods, female gods, mountains and rivers of Tawiniya.

§47 (ii 48–49) Sun-god(dess) of Washaniya, male gods, female gods, mountains and rivers of Washaniya.

§48 (ii 50–51) Lord of Lanta, male gods, female gods, mountains and rivers of Lanta; male gods, female gods, mountains and rivers of Hattina.

§49 (ii 52–54) Male gods, female gods, mountains and rivers of Harpisa. Karmahi of Kalimuna, male gods, female gods, mountains and rivers of Kalimuna.

§50 (ii 55) Male gods, female gods, mountains and rivers of Hakpisa.

§51 (ii 56) Protective-god of the Field, Protective-god of the King, male gods and female gods of His Majesty's grandfather.

§52 (ii 57) Male gods and female gods of His Majesty's father.

§53 (ii 58) Male gods and female gods of His Majesty's grandmother.

§54 (ii 59) Male gods and female gods of the House of Gazzimara.

§55 (ii 60–61) Hatahha of Ankuwa, Storm-god of the Rain, Ishtar of the Field, male gods, female <gods>, mountains and rivers of Ankuwa.

§56 (ii 62–63) Pirwa of Nenisakuwa, Pirwa of Duruwaduruwa, Pirwa of Iksuna.

§57 (ii 64–65) Ishtar of Sulama, Storm-god of Hatra, male gods, female gods, mountains and rivers of the Land of Isuwa.

§58 (ii 66–67) Storm-god of Tegarama, male gods, female gods, mountains and rivers of the Land of Tegarama.

§59 (ii 68) Queen of Paliya.

§60 (ii 69–70) Storm-god of Tupazziya, male gods, female gods, mountains and rivers of Tupazziya.

§61 (ii 71) Karuna of Kariuna.

§62 (ii 72–73) Storm-god of the Growth, Storm-god and Hebat of Apzisna, male gods and female gods of Apzisna.

§63 (iii 1) Protective-god of Kalasmitta.

§64 (iii 2–3) Tamisiya of Tapiqqa, male gods, female gods, mountains and rivers of Tapiqqa.

§65 (iii 4–12) Storm-god of the House of the *tawannanna*, Storm-god *ḫulassassis*, male gods and female gods of the king and the queen who have been invoked and who have not been invoked, to whose temples the king and queen attend and to whose temples they do not attend, but priests make offerings to them, male gods and female gods of the sky and of the dark netherworld, heaven and earth, clouds and winds, thunder and lightning, place of assembly, at which place the gods are wont to assemble.

Invocation of the Sun-god of Heaven, Supreme Judge

§66 (iii 13–17) Sun-god of Heaven, my lord, shepherd of mankind! You, Sun-god of Heaven, arise from the sea, and you take your stand in heaven.[11] Sun-god of Heaven, my lord! You, Sun-god, give daily judgment over man, dog, pig, and the beast of the field.

§67 (iii 18–22) Here am I, Muwatalli the king, priest of the Sun-goddess of Arinna and of all the gods, pleading with the Sun-god of Heaven. Sun-god of Heaven, my lord, halt the gods on this day! And these gods whom I have summoned with my tongue on this day, in whatever plea,

§68 (iii 23–24) summon them, Sun-god of Heaven, from heaven and earth, from mountains and rivers, from their temples and their thrones!

Invocation of the Storm-god of Lightning

§69 (iii 25–31) Thereafter the king says as follows: Storm-god of Lightning, my lord, I was but a human, whereas my father was a priest to the Sun-goddess of Arinna and to all the gods. My father begat me, but the Storm-god of of Lightning took me from my mother and reared me; he made me priest to the Sun-goddess of Arinna and to all the gods; for the Hatti land he appointed me to kingship.

§70 (iii 32–39) So now I, Muwatalli the king, who have been reared by you, by the Storm-god of Lightning, am pleading: The gods whom I have invoked with my tongue and have pleaded to them, intercede for me with these gods, with all of them! Take the words of my tongue, that of Muwatalli, your servant, and transmit them before the gods! The words of prayer which I will present to the gods, let them not turn them back to me!

§71 (iii 40–44) The bird takes refuge in the cage and it lives.[12] I, too, have taken refuge with the Storm-god of Lightning and he has kept me alive. The plea which I make to the gods, transmit its words to the gods, and let them listen to me! Then, I too shall constantly praise the Storm-god of Lightning.

§72 (iii 45–59) When the gods will hear my word, the bad thing which is in my soul, the gods will put it right and remove it from me. A cause of praise for whom will I be? Will I not be the occasion for praise of the Storm-god of Lightning, my lord? And when a god or a human will look, he will say as follows: "Surely, the Storm-god of Lightning, my lord, king of Heaven, has honored the man, has promoted him, has provided for him, and has brought him to (good) times." And in the future it will come to pass that my son, my grandson, kings and queens of Hatti, princes and lords, will always show reverence towards the Storm-god of Lightning, my lord, and they will say as follows: "Truly that god is a mighty hero, a rightly guiding god!" The gods of heaven, the mountains and the rivers will praise you.

§73 (iii 60–70) As for me, Muwatalli, your servant, my soul will rejoice inside me, and I will exalt the Storm-god of Lightning. The temples that I will erect for you and the rites that I will perform for you, Storm-god of Lightning, my lord, you shall rejoice in them. The thick bread and the libations which I constantly offer to the Storm-god of Lightning, my lord, let me offer it to him (B: to you) joyfully, let me not offer it to you reluctantly! Storm-god of Lightning, glow over me like the moonlight, shine over me like the Sun-god of Heaven!

§74 (iii 71-iv 2) Walk with me at my right hand, team up with me as with a bull to draw! Ascend with me in true Storm-godly fashion! Truly, let me say as follows: "I have been recognized, reared and favored by the Storm-god of Lightning, and [. . .]." When he finishes ca[lling the gods (?)], he [. . .]s [. . .].

Ritual Offerings for the Gods of Hatti

§75 (B i 39)[13] [Three] sacrificial breads for the Sun-god of Heaven, ditto.

§76 (iv 3) Thereafter he breaks the thick breads.

§77 (iv 4–7) [. . .], three thick breads of a handful of moist flour to the Sun-goddess of Arinna; he dips them in the honey mixed with fine oil and puts them on the table of the Sun-goddess of Arinna. Thereafter he pours out fat-bread and groats upon the thick breads. He libates in front of them one pitcher of wine.

§78 (iv 8–12) Thereafter, for the Storm-god of Lightning he breaks three white thick breads and one red; he dips them in the honey mixed with fine oil and puts them on the table of the Storm-god of Lightning. Thereafter he pours out groats and fat-bread upon the thick breads. He libates in front of them one pitcher of wine.

§79 (iv 13–17) Thereafter, for Hebat he breaks three white thick breads and one red; he dips them in the honey mixed with fine oil and puts them on the table of Hebat. Thereafter he pours out fat-bread and groats upon the thick breads. He libates in front of them one pitcher of wine.

§80 (iv 18–22) Thereafter he breaks three white thick breads and one red, for the Storm-god of Heaven; he dips them in the honey mixed with fine oil. He puts them on the table of the Storm-god of Heaven. Thereafter he pours out fat-bread and groats upon the thick breads. He libates in front of them one pitcher of wine.

§81 (iv 23–27) Thereafter he breaks three thick breads of a handful of moist flour to the Storm-god of Hatti; he dips them in the honey mixed with fine oil. He puts them on the table of the Storm-god of Hatti. Thereafter he pours out fat-bread and groats upon the thick breads. He libates in front of them one pitcher of wine.

§82 (iv 28–32) Thereafter he breaks three white thick breads and one red, for the Storm-god of Ziplanda; he dips them in honey mixed with fine oil. He puts them on the table of the Storm-god of Zippalanda. Thereafter he pours out fat-bread and groats upon the thick breads. He libates in front of them one pitcher of wine.

§83 (iv 33–35) Thereafter he breaks three white thick breads and one red, for all the male gods of Hatti. He puts them on the table of the Storm-god of Lightning.

§84 (iv 36–37) Thereafter he breaks three white thick breads and one red, for Seri and Hurri. Ditto. He puts them on the table of the Storm-god of Lightning.

§85 (iv 38–40) Thereafter he breaks three white thick breads and one red, for all the female gods of Hatti. Ditto. He puts them on the table of the Sun-goddess of Arinna.

§86 (iv 41–42) Thereafter he breaks three white thick breads and one red, for the mountains. Ditto. He puts them on the table of the Storm-god of Lightning.

§87 (iv 43–44) Thereafter he breaks three white thick breads and one red, for the rivers. Ditto. He puts them on the table of the Storm-god of Lightning.

Insert Personal Prayer Here!

§88 (iv 45–48) When he finishes breaking the thick breads, the things which are in His Majesty's heart, he makes them into a plea to the gods. When the presentation of the plea is finished,

Ritual Offerings for the Gods of All the Lands and the Witness Sun-god

§89 (iv 49–51) thereafter he breaks three white thick breads and one red, for the male gods of all the lands. He pours out fat-bread and groats. He pours out honey mixed with fine oil. He libates one pitcher of wine.

§90 (iv 52–54) Thereafter he breaks three white thick breads and one red, for the female gods of all the lands, to whom he presented a plea. He pours out groats upon the thick breads. He pours out honey mixed with fine oil.

§91 (iv 55) Thereafter he breaks two thick breads for the mountains and rivers (B: of the lands). Ditto.

§92 (iv 56–58) Thereafter he breaks one thick bread for the Witness[14] Sun-god. He pours out fat-bread and groats upon the thick breads. He pours out in front of them honey mixed with fine oil.

Postscript (Only in A): Burning of the Ritual Offerings.

§93 (iv 59–61) Further, they make two fireplaces of wood, and the breads which he breaks, he burns in front of the same two tables. Complete.

Notes

1. The view held by other commentators (Houwink ten Cate/Josephson 1967: 101f.; Lebrun 1980: 305f.), according to which the deterioration of Kummanni was caused by an invasion of the Kaska tribes from the north, has no foundation in the text itself. See Singer 1996: 163.

2. The exact meaning of the positive condition *tarawiya-* (marked as a Luwian gloss) is not known. Suggested renderings include "enrichment," "tranquility," "maturation" (see refs. in HEG III/8: 156).

3. The text has the unclear form NI EŠ.

4 For this sense of the compound GIŠ.HUR *gulzatar* (rather than the more common rendering as "wooden tablets"), see Marazzi 1994: 155f.

5. Cf. *CHD* L–N: 363a. For the rendering of the compound A.ŠÀ A.GÀR as "fallow land," see Hoffner 1997: 191.

6. A typically Kizzuwatnean purification shrine, usually located on a mountain; see literature cited in Singer 1996: 56.

7. The meaning of this phrase is obscure. The "evil bird" probably refers to an unfavorable bird oracle (cf. Engelhard 1970: 55), and MUŠEN.DÙ-*it* could alternatively be a verb describing the action of an "augur."

8. For the restoration and interpretation of this passage, see Singer 1996: 162f.

9. For the reading of this name, see Singer 1996: 162, n. 353.

10. In *B* this list follows after the ritual offerings (§§89–92).

11. *A* has here a Hittite word (*kutrui*), whereas *B* a Luwian one (*huwaialli*).

VI

Prayers of Hattusili, Puduhepa, and Tudhaliya

The period commencing with the peace treaty with Egypt is often designated as the age of *Pax Hethitica*. Indeed, Hattusili and Puduhepa carried out a successful foreign policy, which stabilized, for a while, the long borders of the Hittite Empire (see, e.g., Houwink ten Cate 1996). However, on the inner front, the civil war against Urhi-Tessub and the moral consequences of Hattusili's usurpation of the throne weighed heavily on Hittite conscience and eventually contributed to the ruin of the kingdom. The problem of dynastic legitimation dominated the political agenda of the last generations of Hittite kings, as demonstrated by many political and religious texts.

Prayers composed in this age provide a vivid picture of the growing preoccupation with intrigues and purgings at the royal court, distantly recalling the troubled days of the late Old Kingdom. The earliest of this group of texts seems to be CTH 297.7 (A. KUB 31.66 + IBoT 3.122; B. HT 7), a text probably composed by (or in the name of) Urhi-Tessub/Mursili III (Houwink ten Cate 1974: 129–136; 1994: 240–243). The very fragmentary text is directed to the Sun-goddess of Arinna and to the Storm-god of Hatti and may indeed belong to a penitential prayer (idem, 1974 135, n. 39), though others have classified it as a trial protocol (Laroche, CTH 297; see further Introduction).

Similar exculpation of problematic legal actions characterizes the prayer of Hattusili (no. 21). As an all-purpose mitigating circumstance for possible past sins, both he and his wife (no. 22) refer to the liberation of Nerik and the restitution of its cult. On the theological level, there is a deliberate departure from Muwatalli's reform centered on the Storm-god of Lightning, and a return to the dominance of the great goddesses of Anatolia—the Sun-goddess of Arinna, Hebat of Kummanni, and Ishtar/

Sausga of Samuha—and their children, Sarruma and the Storm-god of Nerik/ Zippalanda (Singer 1998: 540). Questions of dynastic legitimacy still haunt Tudhaliya IV (Archi 1971: 212; Bryce 1998: 332ff.), but his poorly preserved prayer (nos. 24) seem to be more concerned with cultic issues and with the enemy threat.

No. 21
Hattusili's Prayer of Exculpation
to the Sun-goddess of Arinna
CTH 383

This plea is probably the most "political" Hittite prayer, providing an invaluable list of suspected offences from the days of Mursili onwards, including: Mursili's case against Tawannanna (§2); Muwatalli's transfer of the capital to Tarhuntassa (§3'); Muwatalli's case against Danuhepa and her sons (§4'); the enthronement of Urhi-Tessub by Hattusili (§5'); and the resulting civil war between the two (§6'ff.). The piety and self-sacrifice of Hattusili in the matter of Nerik is accentuated in contrast to Urhi-Tessub's betrayal of the gods (§5'). The Sun-goddess of Arinna is expected to amply reciprocate the favors bestowed upon her son, the Storm-god of Nerik. The single manuscript, inscribed on a double-column tablet, has been augmented by several new fragments, including 1193/u (for which see Singer 2002a). Remarkably, both this prayer and Puduhepa's (no. 22) have no colophon.

Hymn to the Sun-goddess of Arinna

§1 (i 1–13) To the Sun-goddess of Arinna, my lady, lady of the Hatti lands, queen of heaven and earth, lady of the kings and queens of Hatti, torch of the Hatti land. You are the one who rules the kings and queens of Hatti. The one whom you look on with favor as king or queen is right with you, O Sun-goddess of Arinna, my lady. You are the one who chooses and the one who abandons. Contrary to the other gods, you took for yourself as your share the Hatti lands, out of esteem for the Storm-god of Nerik, the Storm-god of Zippalanda, your son.

Plea Concerning the Sins of Former Kings

§2 (i 14–40) Hattusili, your servant and Puduhepa, your maid, have made this plea as follows: Whenever my father, Mursili, while still alive, offended the gods, my lords, by some deed, I was in no way involved in that deed of my father; I was still a child. When the case against Tawannanna, your maid, took place in the palace, how my father curtailed the power of Tawannanna, the queen, though she was the servant of the deity, you, O goddess, my lady, were the one who knew in [your] soul, [whether the curtailing of the power of the queen] was your wish [or whether it] was [not your wish. He caused] the curtailing of the power [of Tawannanna, but I was not involved in the matter] at all. It was [a matter of compulsion for me. If the goddess, my lady, is] somehow [angry about that matter, then] the one who conducted [that case against Tawannanna has already died (lit.: has become a god). He stepped down from the road and has already paid for it] with his head. [But I] was not involved [in that decree. I was still a child. O Sun-goddess] of Arinna, my lady, [do not protract that affair against me. To protract such a thing against me during my days is not right]. *Small break.*

§3' (i 1'–15') . . . he] moved. Whether the trans[fer of the gods was] in accordance with the wish [of the Sun-goddess of Arinna, my lady, or whether it] was [not in accordance with your] wish, you, [my lady,] are the one who knew [that in your soul, O Goddess, my lady. But I was not] involved [in that] order of the trans[fer] of the gods [in any way]. [For me it was a matter] of compulsion, [because] he was my master. But [the transfer] of the gods was not in accordance with my wish, and I was rather worried concerning that [order]. Concerning the silver and the gold of all the gods [. . .], to which god he gave whose silver and gold, in that decision, too, I was not [involved] in any way.

§4' (i 16'-ii 22) When it came to pass that the case against Danuhepa, your priestess, took place in the palace, [how he curtailed the power of] Danuhepa until she was ruined together with her sons and all her men, lords and subordinates, that which was inside the soul of the goddess, my lady, nobody knew, namely, whether the ruination of Danuhepa was the wish of the Sun-goddess of Arinna,[my lady], or whether it was not her wish. In any case, I was not involved in that matter of the ruination of Danuhepa's son. On the contrary, when I passed judgement over him, he was dear to me. Nobody was destroyed by the order of the word of my mouth. The one who did that evil thing—if somehow the Sun-goddess of Arinna, my lady, became angry over the matter of Danuhepa—that one who did that matter of Danuhepa has already died (lit.: has become a god). He stepped down from the road and paid for it with his head. O Sun-goddess of Arinna, my lady ! Do not drag up again the matter of

Danuhepa against me and the land of Hatti during my days! To drag up again such a thing against me during my days is not right.[1] The one who has carried out the matter of Danuhepa, that one has already paid for it himself.

§5' (ii 23–40) When Muwatalli, my brother, died (lit.: became god), out of esteem for my brother I did nothing. I took Urhi-Tessub, my brother's son, and I installed him in kingship. Whether it was the wish of the gods, or whether it [was] not your [wish], I did that thing out of respect for my brother. [I took] my brother's son and I installed him to kingship. But he [. . .] of the Sun-goddess of Arinna, and he betrayed[2] you (pl.) [. . .]. Father, grandfather [. . .]. He did that [. . .] and to you offering bread [. . .] the temples not [. . .] of silver [. . .]. You(pl.) [. . .] that thing [. . .]

Broken. The end of obv. ii and the beginning of rev. iii is perhaps provided by Bo 4222.

(Bo 4222 obv. 1'–8') [. . .] to you (pl.) grandmothers [. . .] some (evil) tongue away [. . .] he kept praying [. . .] evil [thing . . .] since [. . .] your (pl.) priest, your (pl.) servant [. . .]

§6' (Bo 4222 rev. 1'–11') [. . .] gods [. . .] I, to the gods [. . .] was [. . .] I [did not . . .] him/her [. . . and] I did not do evil at all. [. . .] My wife [. . .] for me before the gods [. . .]. [. . .] a blood-relation of mine [. . .] put down in front of yourselves [and investigate it(?) . . .] he/she killed [. . .]he/she himself died [. . .] *Broken.*[3]

Hattusili's Dedication to Nerik

§7' (iii 2'–8') But I, Hattusili, [your servant, . . .] in the place in which [. . .] I have put [. . .] of the Storm-god of Nerik, and how [. . .] in, and how he reached(?) me entirely(?)[. . .], you did not [. . .], O Sun-goddess of Arinna, my lady.

§8' (iii 9'–25') When my brother, Muwatalli, [gave] me Hattusa [. . .], the city of Katapa, as well as other [lands], I refused them.[4] The land of Nerik was suddenly ruined under the former kings, and the roads [were] thickly wooded. The city of Nerik was like a stone[5] in the [sea(?)]; it [was] under deep water. I brought the city of Nerik up like a stone out of deep water. I [picked it] up for the sake of the Storm-god of Nerik, your son. I resettled the land of Nerik and I rebuilt [the city of] Nerik. For [the sake] of the land of Nerik I engaged my body and soul. Those who were kings in the past, and to whom the Storm-god had given the weapon, kept defeating the enemies, but no one recaptured the land of Nerik, and no one rebuilt it.

§9' (iii 26"-iv 25') When Urhi-Tessub, who [kept pursuing(?)[6]] me because of the lordship, became alienated from me over the land of Nerik, my friends and associates kept intimidating[7] me saying: "For Nerik you will perish." I listened neither to my lord's anger nor to the intimidation of my associates. I heard this [. . .] and I heard this [. . .], and I said as follows: "Before I give Nerik to another let me rather die for Nerik !" I was but a human but I did not toil for human wealth. I did not seek wealth(?).[8] Rather, I [. . .] the land of yours, O Goddess, for the sake of your son. And as I, a human, did it, namely, took the beloved place of the Storm-god of Nerik, your son, the city of Nerik, O Sun-goddess of Arinna, my lady, lady of the Hatti lands, O Storm-god of Hatti, my lord, do this thing for the sake of the matter of the Storm-god of Nerik, your beloved son! If before the gods there is some sin of my father and my mother, or if it is [some(?)] ancient sin,[9] and you goddess, my lady, pursue it [. . .], disregard that sin, O Goddess, my lady, for the sake of the Storm-god of Nerik, your beloved [son]. Do not [. . .] it. For the gods the *dahanga*[10] is a place of mercy. O Sun-goddess of Arinna, lady[11] of the Hatti lands, take it to your confident(?) heart in the *dahanga,* the place of mercy ! If there are sins in Hatti, whatever they are, disregard them indeed, O Sun-goddess of Arinna, my lady, for the sake of the matter of the *dahanga*! Even if a human being raises a child for its father and mother, doesn't the father and mother pay him/her what is due to a wetnurse, and doesn't he rejoice over it?[12] I have also labored for the city of the Storm-god of Nerik, your beloved son. Spare my soul and the soul of my wife and my children, O Sun-goddess of Arinna, [my lady, for the sake of the city] of the Storm-god of Nerik, your beloved son! Re[press] that evil for [. . .]. [. . .] for myself, my wife [. . .], [. . .] he is alienated [. . .] of the Storm-god of Arinna [. . .] of your son [. . .] *Break.*

§10' (iv 3'-11') *Only line ends preserved. Arinna (l. 9') and Hattusa, the place of assembly of the gods (l. 10'f.), are mentioned.*

§11' (iv 12'-28') *First two lines almost entirely broken.* [And if] those sins somehow still exist before the gods, and some god has been invoked on account of that evil matter and he attends to it, then as soon as the Storm-god and the gods gather to the assembly, and someone speaks concurrently about that evil matter in the assembly, then the Sun-goddess of Arinna, the Storm-god of Hatti and the gods should take to their heart the matter of the *dahanga* of the Storm-god of Nerik. O Sun-goddess of

Arinna and gods [of] Hatti, repress that evil thing from there! May Hattusa, the place of assembly of the gods, Arinna, your beloved city, and Nerik and Zippalanda, the cities of your son, be distinguished for you.[13]
End of text. Tablet ends with free space. There is no colophon.

No. 22
Puduhepa's Prayer to the Sun-goddess of Arinna and her Circle for the Well-being of Hattusili
(CTH 384)

Puduhepa is no doubt the best-known Hittite queen (Darga 1974; Otten 1975). Daughter of a Kizzuwatnean priest, she was extremely influential in state affairs, both on the side of her husband Hattusili and, after his death, as the dowager queen on the side of her son Tudhaliya. In her capacity as chief priestess of the kingdom she organized a comprehensive revision of state religion, promoting in particular the cult of the great goddesses of Anatolia, whom she sought to syncretize with each other (§2).

As frankly stated in his autobiography (see van den Hout 1997: 101; §3), from birth Hattusili suffered from ill health which seems to have dogged him throughout his life. Puduhepa's genuine concern over her spouse's illness is demonstrated by her vows (Otten/Souček 1969) and by this plea dedicated to his well-being. She first turns to the Sun-Goddess of Arinna, alias Hebat, and reminds her of Hattusili's dedication to the cause of Nerik, the abode of her beloved son, which no king before him managed to recapture. She enhances the effect of this argument by referring to a folk saying: "to a woman of the birthstool the deity grants her wish" (§§6, 15"; Fontaine 1987). The term may be understood as referring to a woman who had given birth herself (Pringle 1983: 136), as well as to one assisting at another's delivery, viz. a midwife (Beckman 1983a: 233f.). According to her own testimony, Puduhepa was particularly skilled in both capacities (see Beckman 1996: 128, §11).

After pleading with the main goddess, Puduhepa turns to four deities of her entourage to intercede with the main gods for the health of Hattusili: Liliwani (Lelwani), goddess of the Netherworld (cf. no. 15); Zintuhi, granddaughter of the Sun-Goddess and the Storm-god; Mezzulla, their daughter; and the Storm-god of Zippalanda, their son, who is equated with the Storm-god of Nerik (no. 23, §1; Haas 1970: 107ff.; Popko 1994: 33). To each of these deities she vows a special present if her wish is fulfilled: a lifesize silver statue of Hattusili, an exquisite jewel, an estate including serfs, and a golden shield, respectively. As in Hattusili's prayer (no. 21), the single manuscript, inscribed on a double-column tablet, has no colophon (cf. also no. 20).

Prayer and Vow to the Sun-goddess of Arinna

§1 (i 1–2) To the Sun-goddess of Arinna, my lady, lady of the Hatti lands, queen of heaven and earth:

§2 (i 3–33) O Sun-goddess of Arinna, my lady, queen of all the lands! In Hatti you gave yourself the name Sun-goddess of Arinna, but the land which you made, that of the cedar, there you gave yourself the name Hebat. I, Puduhepa, am your long-time servant, a calf of your stable, a (corner)stone of your foundation. You picked me up, my lady, and Hattusili, your servant, to whom you married me, and he too was attached by destiny (lit. lot) to the Storm-god of Nerik, your beloved son. The place in which you, O Sun-goddess of Arinna, my lady, installed us, is the place of your beloved son, the Storm-god of Nerik. How the former kings neglected it, that you know O Sun-goddess of Arinna, my lady. Those who were former kings, to whom you, O Sun-goddess of Arinna, had given weapons, kept defeating the [surrounding] enemy lands, but no one [tried] to take/[succeeded] in taking the city of Nerik. But he who is your servant, Hattusili, and whom you now [pursue (?)][14], O Sun-goddess of Arinna, my lady, was not even a king, but only a prince. Yet, it was up to him to take the city of Nerik. Had he not succeeded [in capturing] the city of Nerik, his [brother would have handed over] to him other lands.[15] He even(?) gave him Hattusa whole[heartedly(?)], as well as Katapa [but he refused them.(?)][16] O Sun-goddess of Arinna, my lady, [you knew(?)] it [...] the Storm-god of Nerik [...]. *A few lines missing.*

§3' (i 33'–37') [For] the land of Nerik and for the land of [Hakpis(?)] he kept placing [his] body and his [very life] at risk as long as he held the campaign against [the Kaska enemy(?)].[17]

§4' (i 38'–54') But when Muwatalli, [his brother(?)], died (lit.: became god), he[18] took [up] Urhi-Tessub, [his brother's son(?)], and installed him to kingship. How he [oppressed(?)/limited(?)] Hattusili, your servant, in/to Nerik, that you know, O Sun-goddess of Arinna, my lady. His lord kept pursuing him, and the princes kept intimidating him saying: "For Nerik you might [perish]." But he did not consider his own ruin and his own death saying: "For Nerik [I would rather choose(?)] death! And [before I hand(?)] over Nerik [..."

Five more very fragmentary lines and then break.

§5' (ii 1–10) [. . .] we will purify ourselves, [and then] we will carry out the cult for you, O gods, in the same way, and we will observe your regulation and ritual likewise. Since they have stopped [the offerings(?)][19] for you, O gods, they will celebrate the old [yearly] and monthly festivals for the gods. [The offerings(?)] will never be stopped again, O gods, my lords, as long as we, your servant and your maid, carry out the cult.

§6' (ii 11–37) This matter I, Puduhepa, your maid, made into a prayer to the Sun-goddess of Arinna, my lady, lady of the Hatti lands, queen of heaven and earth. Have pity on me, O Sun-goddess of Arinna, my lady, and hear me! Even among humans one often speaks the following saying: "To a woman of the birthstool the deity grants her wish." [Since] I, Puduhepa, am a woman of the birthstool, and I have devoted myself to your son, have pity on me, O Sun-goddess of Arinna, my lady, and grant me what [I ask of you]! Grant life to [Hattusili], your servant! [Through the Fate-goddesses] and the Mother-goddesses may [long] years, days [and strength] be granted to him.[20] [. . .] [an angry (?)[21]] god [. . .] you have. All the gods [. . .] they have [. . . no/some]one calls [. . .]. Request life [for Hattusili], your servant, in the place [of assembly] of all the gods, and may your wish be wholehearted! And since you, O Sun-goddess of Arinna, my lady, have shown favor [to me], [depen]dability(?)[22] and even right [. . .], [. . .] revere[nce(?)] to the will of [the gods(?)]. [Don't] you see, O Sun-goddess of Arinna, my lady, how I [fulfilled(?)] the wish of the Sun-goddess of Arinna, my lady? [. . .] in this matter [. . .], [. . .] the request [do not turn(?)] back.

§7' (ii 38–43) *Only a few signs left (including "daughter-in-law") followed by a break. The beginning of rev. III is almost entirely broken.*

Prayer and Vow to Liliwani

§8" (iii 9'–35') [Liliwani, my lady, whatever] you say [to the gods (?)], they grant [it to you]. Support me [in this matter]! In this thing that I heard [among] men, and before me [the matter was said(?), namely, that] Hattusili, who is your servant, [is ill(?)], what [people] said about him at the time of Urhi-Tessub, namely: "[His years] are short"; now, if Hattusili, your servant, has been defamed before you, O gods, by a human hand, or if any of the Upper gods or the Lower gods has been offended by him, or if anyone has offered to the gods in order to damage Hattusili, you, O Goddess, my lady, do not [listen] to those evil words! Don't let [the evil] get to Hattusili, your servant! [Do not turn us over], O gods,

[my] lords, [to . . . (?)], to our adversaries, [to evil men (?)]! [If] you, O goddess, my lady, keep him alive and speak [favorably] to the gods, and tread with your feet these evil [words], and [. . .] them away, then to you, Liliwani [. . .]. Let [the life(?)] of Hattusili, your servant, and of Puduhepa, your maid, [come forth] from your mouth before the gods! Grant to Hattusili, your servant, and to Puduhepa, [your maid,] long years, months and days!

§9" (iii 36'–42') If you, Liliwani, my lady, will speak favorably [to the gods], and will keep your servant, Hattusili, alive and grant him long years, months and days, I shall come and make for Liliwani, my lady, a silver statue of Hattusili, as big as Hattusili himself, with its head, its hands and its feet of gold; that I will weigh out separately. *Empty space of some 5 lines.*

Prayer and Vow to Zintuhi

§10" (iii 43'–47') O Zintuhi, my lady, beloved granddaughter of the Storm-god and the Sun-goddess of Arinna! You are an ornament on the breast of the Storm-god and of the Sun-goddess of Arinna, and they watch you time after time.

§11" (iv 1'–7') Beginning missing. Zintuhi, my lady, [in this matter express your] providence! To the Storm-god, your grandfather, [and] to the Sun-goddess of Arinna, your grandmother, transmit life and long years for Hattusili, your servant! May it come forth from their mouth!

§12" (8'–12') If you will hear these words Zintuhi, my lady, and you will pass them on to the Storm-god, your grandfather, [and] to the Sun-goddess, your grandmother, I will make for Zintuhi, my lady, a [great] ornament.

Prayer and Vow to Mezzulla

§13" (iv 13'–23') O Mezzulla, my lady, beloved daughter of the Storm-god [and] the Sun-goddess of Arinna! [Whatever] you, Mezzulla, my lady, say to the Storm-god, your father, and to the Sun-goddess of Arinna, your mother, they listen to it indeed. They will not refuse it. These words which I, Puduhepa, your maid, have made into a prayer to the Storm-god, your father, and to the Sun-goddess of Arinna, your mother, announce them for me, O Mezzulla, my lady, and pass them on to the Storm-god, your father, [and] to the Sun-goddess of Arinna, your mother, and intercede on my behalf!

§14" (iv 24'–27') If you Mezzulla, [my lady], will pass [these] words on to the Storm-god, your father, and [to the Sun-goddess of Arinna], your mother, and you will intercede on my behalf, I will give [you towns(?)] including deportees.

Prayer and Vow to the Storm-god of Zippalanda

§15" (iv 28'–47') [O Storm-god] of Zippalanda, my lord, you are the beloved son [of the Storm-god and] the Sun-goddess of Arinna. [Whatever you] announce [to the Storm-god, your father,] and to the Sun-goddess of Arinna, your mother, [the Storm-god], your father, and the Sun-goddess of Arinna, your mother, will [not] refuse your word. They will hear you. This [word] which I, Puduhepa, your maid, [made] into a prayer, announce it for me, O Storm-god of Zippalanda, my lord, and pass it on. Have pity on me in this matter, O god, my lord! Since I am a woman of the birthstool, and I have personally made restitution to the god, my lord, intercede on my behalf, O god, my lord, with [the Storm-god], your father, and with the Sun-goddess of Arinna! Hattusili, your servant, took pains for the god's will, and he engaged his body and soul until he rebuilt Nerik, the beloved city [of] the god, my lord. You, O god, my lord, be favorably inclined towards Hattusili, your servant. And the words which I lay in prayer before the Storm-god, your father, and the Sun-goddess of Arinna, your mother, pass them on for me O Storm-god of Zippalanda, my lord!

§16" (iv 48'-left edge 4) If you, O Storm-god of Zippalanda, my lord, will pass on for me these words to the Storm-god, your father, and to the Sun-goddess of Arinna, your mother, and [you will save] Hattusili from evil [. . .], I shall make [for the Storm-god of Zippalanda], my [lord], a golden shield weighing two minas. I shall make [. . .]; [I will consecrate] to the god [. . .] the town Puputana [. . .], [. . .].

End. There is no colophon.

No. 23
Fragments of Prayers to the Storm-god of Nerik
CTH 386.1–3

The following passages from prayers to the Storm-god of Nerik do not necessarily belong to the same text. Several other texts belonging to the cult of Nerik (CTH 671–678; Haas 1970) contain prayer-like passages incorporated within rituals and festival descriptions (e.g. CTH 671; Lebrun 1980: 375ff.).

The first passage (CTH 386.1) may have been composed by Hattusili on the occcasion of the appointment of Tudhaliya to the office of priest of the Storm-god of Nerik (§1). It evokes the deity from mountains in the region of Nerik (§1) and from various farther localities (§2), which basically cover the entire territory of Anatolia.

The second, hymn-like passage (CTH 386.2) conventionally identifies the mother of the Storm-god of Nerik as the Sun-goddess of Arinna (§3), whereas in the first passage (§1) she is Ereshkigal, the Mesopotamian queen of the Netherworld; the syncretism is obvious.

The third very fragmentary passage (CTH 386.3) seems to list cases in which the supplicant passed over/neglected (*CHD* P: 39) a divine command, for which he must repent.

Evocation

§1 (1'–28') [. . . Storm-god of] Nerik, my lord! [. . .] Zahapuna [. . .]. May (s)he call a sweet [message(?)] like a . . . to the Storm-god of Nerik! May (s)he awaken the Storm-god of Nerik from his sweet dream! May he come, the Storm-god of Nerik! Come, O Storm-god of Nerik, from heaven and earth! Come, O Storm-god of Nerik, from east (lit. sunrise) and west (lit. sunset)! From heaven, if you are with the Storm-god, your father; from earth, if you are in the dark earth with Ereshkigal, your mother. Come at dawn to your festival! At dawn they will anoint Tudhaliya to priesthood in your favorite places, Hakmis and Nerik. Come tomorrow to your festival! Come from Mount Hahruwa, your favorite, to the place where your body and soul are! Come from Mount Zaliyanu, from Mount Harpisa, from Mount Dahalmuna, from Mount Idalhamuna, from Mount Tahali(?), from Mount Tagurta, from Mount [. . .]hulla, from Mount Puskurunuwa, [. . .]. [Come], O Storm-god of Nerik, my lord, from all the mountains! [Come, O Storm-god of Nerik,] my lord, [. . .] from your mountains!

§2 (29'–47') [Come] from the Marassanta River! Come from the *mazumazuwanta*, from the bank! Come from Zalpa, from the sea! Come from the source of Nerik, your favorite! Come from Lihsina, from Mount Lihsina! Come from the east, come from the west! Come from whichever mountain[23] you are on! Come from the Upper Land! Come from the Lower Land! Come from the land of Arzawa! Come from [the Land of]

Hurri! Come from the Land of Kummanni! Come from all the lands! Come from the west side (lit. wind), the north side, the south side, [the east] side]—from the four corners! [. . .] Hakmis [. . .], Nerik, from the lands [. . .], the Land of Hatti [. . .] you have taken your pillar(?) [. . .] unmentioned [. . .] *The rest is almost entirely broken.*

Hymn

The first column is missing.

§1 (ii 1–9) O Storm-god, in all the lands you heal(?) [. . .]. O Storm-god of Nerik, my lord, strong(?) iron [. . .]. Do not call down the well-being of the land! Do not call down the [. . . of] mankind! Do not call down the [mild(?)] rains! Evoke the [. . .] of the land! [. . .] your mother's lapis lazuli [. . .] sweet dreams [. . .]" *Broken.*

§2 (iii 1'–3') You govern [the *labarna*(?),] the king, the *tawananna*, [the queen(?). . .]

§3 (iii 4–8) [If] something burdens the *labarna*, the king [. . .], [may(?)] the roads of the [dark] earth be open to you! [May(?)] the roads [. . .] be left for you [. . .]. [. . .] to you, your <<grand>>father is the Storm-god [. . .]; your [mother] is the Sun-goddess of Arinna; the heaven is [your] house [. . .]. *End of column. Fourth column is lost.*

Confession

From col. ii only traces of ends of lines are left; the top of col. iii is missing too.

§1 (iii 1'–10') [. . .] I stood up, and I returned to Nerik to sacrifice to the gods. When some weapon was given to me by the god, and whoever revolted against me, I neglected that place.

§2 (iii 11'–22') When later some year again arrived and struck my eyes through an oracle, I neglected that too. I did not consult an oracle [. . .] as follows: "This [. . .] because to Nerik I did [not(?)] go? *The rest is broken. The top of col. iv is missing.*

§3 (iv 2'–22) The Storm-god of Nerik [. . .] is angry(?), words [. . .] he has. I neglected them in [. . .] will(?), and I have brought them in order to you, O Storm-god of Nerik, [my lord]. [But] since he is angry against me, I have made a plea from afar. Speak across for your beloved son, O Storm-god, my lord, and intercede for me!

The rest of this paragraph and the next one are too fragmentary for translation. Mention is made of "ancestors" and "the place of the god."

No. 24
Tudhaliya's Prayer to the Sun-goddess of Arinna for Military Success
(CTH 385.9)

This fragmentary prayer is one of the rare contributions of Tudhaliya IV to the genre. In the first and only relatively well-preserved paragraph, the king admits his sin in neglecting the festivals of the Sun-goddess. He solemnly vows to perform them in time, and petitions the deity's assistance in defeating the enemy. In the second, very fragmentary paragraph the cause for the wrath of the goddess seems to be anchored somehow "in the days of Suppiluliuma" (l. 12), who is known to have neglected some cults (no. 11, §3). In the last paragraph the king vows to build a temple for the Sun-goddess in Arinna and to offer to her thousands (of sacrificial animals?) on Mount Tagurka (near Hanhana). The identity of the enemy whose defeat is requested is not indicated, but Tudhaliya is known to have faced serious threats on all fronts, notably against the Assyrians (Singer 1985; Bryce 1998: 326ff.).

§1 (obv. 1–10) [. . .] Tudhaliya has made [a plea] as follows: I have sinned [against the Sun-goddess of Arinna], my lady, and I have offended the Sun-goddess of Arinna, [my lady]. [And when] I began to get oracular guidance, (it turned out that) I neglected your festivals. [If you], O Sun-goddess of Arinna, my lady, became angry with [me] on account of some festivals, take care [of me] again, O Sun-goddess of Arinna, my lady! May I defeat the enemy! [If you, O Sun-goddess] of Arinna, my lady, will step down [to me], and I shall defeat the enemy, I shall [confess] my sin [before you] and never again [shall I omit] the festivals. I will not again interchange the spring and [autumn festivals]. [The festivals of spring] I shall perform only in the spring, [and the festivals of] autumn I shall perform only in the autumn. I shall never leave out [the festivals(?)] in [your] temple.

The next paragraph of the obverse (§2) and the first preserved paragraphs of the reverse (§§3'–4') are too fragmentary for translation. The mention of Suppilu[liuma] in obv. 12 seems to be related to the wrath of the gods in the previous line.

§5' (rev. 11'–15') [. . .] for me Mount Tagurka I shall [. . .], and I shall make for you in Arinna [a new(?)] temple. [. . .]. [When] I, My Majesty, [will set out] to return for the winter festivals, and if I shall defeat the enemy, when I return from the battle-field, I shall go up to Mount

Tagurka, and I shall give you thousands [. . .], and I shall make reparation. *The text probably does not have a colophon.*

Notes

1. Despite the unusual form, *natta arān* is probably the same as *natta ara*, "not right" (contra Ünal 1973: 142, n. 106). For this expression, see Cohen 1997; 2002.

2. Lit. "rubbed your chest.: See *CHD*, P: 205.

3. Marazzi 1983: 332 suggests that this passage may refer to the affair of Arma-Tarhunta, for which see Hattusili's Autobiography, §10a (iii 24–30); van den Hout 1997: 104; Bryce 1998; 274.

4. So with Sürenhagen 1981: 95. Marazzi 1983: 332 and *CHD*, L–N: 384b render this phrase as a rhetorical question: ". . . did I refuse them?" The parallel passage in the Puduhepa prayer (no. 22 no. 21, §2) is damaged, but it also seems to convey that Hattusili did *not* accept any other city (including Hattusa) instead of his beloved Nerik (Singer 2001).

5. The word *aku-* (with the stone determinative) is translated by some as "seashell" (e.g., *CHD*, L–N: 101b), but since it is also used to describe roads, the sense "stone, pebble" seems preferable (Sürenhagen 1981: 106f.).

6. Restored after no. 21, §4' (i 44'). Güterbock 1988: 115 restores "quarrelled."

7. The correct reading in iii 31" is *kurkuriškir* (not *šarriškir*). See Hoffner 1980: 202a; Marazzi 1983: 332; Güterbock 1988.

8. Assuming the omission of NÍG before TUKU.

9. So after Otten 1958: 118. Sürenhagen 1981: 96 restores "sin of ancient [kings]."

10. The cult room of the temple of the Storm-god of Nerik. See Haas 1970: 90f.; 1994: 601; Sürenhagen 1981: 107f.

11. The text has "my lady," but the best way to render the whole sentence is by omitting the superfluous "my." Cf. Sürenhagen 1981: 97, who takes the Hatti Lands to be the object of the sentence.

12. Similarly Archi 1971: 196, n. 37 and Sürenhagen 1981: 97. Somewhat differently Hoffner 1973: 113f.

13. Lit. "be seen." Other renderings of the last sentence: Sürenhagen 1981: 99: "Let *a*, *b*, *c*, and *d* be considered as the cities of your son!"; Houwink ten Cate 1987: 22: "And Hattusa should count for you (i.e., be reckoned with by you) . . . !"

14. The sign *ša-* before the break should probably be restored as a verb: *sakuwai-* "see" (Sürenhagen 1981: 110), *sak-* "know" (van den Hout 1995: 1113), or, most likely, *sanh-*, "seek, pursue, test" (cf. Hatt. §9"=KUB 14.7 iv 2).

15. For this restoration of the passage, cf., e.g., KBo 6.29 i 24, 30 (Götze 1925: 46; *CHD*, L–N 166a). For other restorations, cf. Ünal 1973: 73, n. 127; 1991: 814; Sürenhagen 1981: 110; Marazzi 1983: 337, 340.

16. Restored after the parallel passage in the Hattusili prayer, no. 21 §8. See Singer 2001.

17. So with Archi 1971: 191 ᴸ[ᵁKÚR *Kaska*]. Goetze 1950: 393; Sürenhagen

1981: 110; Ünal 1991: 814; Hoffner 1997: 206 and *CHD* 3: 278, restore LU[GAL KUR ᵁᴿᵁ*Mizri*], "k[ing of Egypt]."

18. The verbal form (*datta*) is both second- and third-person singular. In the former case, which is preferred by most commentators, it is the goddess who installed Urhi-Tessub on the throne. But on the force of the comparison with Hattusili's Autobiography (III 41f.), it seems preferable that Puduhepa refers here to her own husband who put Urhi-Tessub on the throne.

19. Van den Hout 1998: 226f. (quoting H. A. Hoffner) restores here and in the next sentence "gods," providing parallels for "locking up gods," i.e., putting an end to their cult.

20. The Fate-goddesses and the Mother-goddesses appear as midwives in the Song of Ullikummi (Hoffner 1990: 53 §12).

21. Sürenhagen 1981: 112 (followed by Ünal 1991: 815) suggests *genz*]*uwalaš*, "merciful," but the traces left repudiate this restoration. *karp*]*iwalaš*, "angry," is possible, but not certain.

22. Perhaps [*hapanz*]*uwalatar*, as suggested by Marazzi 1983: 338.

23. So with Lebrun 1980: 369, rather than "from Mount Kuwapita" (Haas 1970: 179), which is nowhere else attested.

Sources

Early Invocations

1. Invocation of the Sun-goddess of the Netherworld against Slander
   Text: CTH 371: KBo 7.28 + KBo 8.92.
   Edition: Friedrich 1957; Lebrun 1980: 83–91.
   Translation: Bernabé 1987: 251–253; Christmann-Franck 1989: 41–42; Ünal 1991: 793–795.
   Discussion: Güterbock 1978: 127–128; de Roos 1995: 2000–2001.

2. Invocation of the Sun-god and the Storm-god against Slander
   Text: CTH 389.2: A. KUB 36.91 (+) KUB 43.68. B. KUB 60.156. C. 871/z (ZA 64: 243f.). D. 702/z (ZA 84: 290).
   Edition: Lebrun 1980: 392–396; Otten/Rüster 1975: 243–244 (partial).
   Discussion: Van den Hout 1998: 74.

3. Invocation of the Sun-goddess of Arinna for the Protection of the Royal Couple
   Text: CTH 385.10: A. KUB 57.63. B. KUB 57.60.
   Edition: Archi 1988.
   Translation: Haas 1994: 430.

Early Empire Prayers

4. Prayers to the Sun-god for Appeasing an Angry God
4a. Prayer of Kantuzzili
   Text: CTH 373: A. KUB 30.10. B. KBo 25.111.
   Edition: Güterbock 1958: 237–243; 1974; 1978: 132–134; Lebrun 1980: 111–120; Görke 2000.

Translation: Goetze 1950: 400–401; Kühne 1978: 167–169; Bernabé 1987: 259–262.
Discussion: Marazzi/Nowicki 1978; Marazzi 1983: 325–326; Carruba 1983: 11; Catsanicos 1991: 9–11; Klinger/Neu 1990: 148–149; Wilhelm 1994: 61–68; Cohen 1997: 69–72; 2002: 44–49.

4b. Prayer of a King
  Text: CTH 374: 1. KBo 34.22 + KUB 31.135 + KUB 30.11 (+) KUB 31.130 + Bo 9659 (AoF 6: 74, n. 36; join Görke 2000). 2.A. KUB 36.75 + Bo 4696 (ZA 62: 231) + 1226/u (ZA 67: 56). 2.B. KBo 22.75 (+) 1698/u (+) 221/w (ZA 64: 241f.). 2.C. KUB 31.134. 3. KUB 31.129.
  Edition: Güterbock 1958: 237–243; 1974; 1978: 132–134; 1980: 42; Lebrun 1980: 121–131; Görke 2000.
  Discussion: Marazzi/Nowicki 1978; Marazzi 1983: 325; Carruba 1983: 11; Klinger/Neu 1990: 148–149; Wilhelm 1994: 61–68.

4c. Prayer of a Mortal
  Text: CTH 372: A. KUB 31.127 + KUB 36.79 + ABoT 44 + FHG 1 + ABoT 44b + ABoT 44a + KUB 31.131 + KUB 31.132 + KUB 36.79a + KBo 38.165 (StBoT 42: 81, 229). B. KUB 31.128. [C = no. 8] D. KUB 31.133. [E = no. 8] F. KBo 14.74. G. KUB 43.67.
  Edition: Güterbock 1958: 237–243; 1974; 1978: 130–134; Lebrun 1980: 92–111; Görke 2000.
  Translation: Christmann-Franck 1989: 42–47; Ünal 1991: 796–799.
  Discussion: Otten 1958: 123f.; Marazzi/Nowicki 1978; Marazzi 1983: 325; Carruba 1983: 11; Klinger/Neu 1990: 148–149; Wilhelm 1994: 61–68; Košak 1998: 81, 229.

5. Prayer of Arnuwanda and Asmunikal to the Sun-goddess of Arinna about the Ravages of the Kaska
  Text: CTH 375: 1. A. KUB 17.21 + 545/u + 578/u + 1619/u + 768/v. B. KUB 31.124 + 1691/u + Bo 8617 + KUB 48.28. C. KUB 23.115 + KUB 23.17 + KUB 31.117 (+) 1398/u + 1945/u (+) 1241/u (+) 766/v + Bo 69/484. D. KUB 31.72 + KUB 48.107 (+) KUB 48.110. E. Bo 2525. F. 398/u + 1945/u. G. HFAC 72. H. KUB 48.108. 2. KUB 31.123 + FHL 3. 3. KBo 12.132. 4. A. 1691/u. B. 1241/u + 766/v. 5. 1099/u + 1095/u.
  Edition: von Schuler 1965: 152–167; Lebrun 1980: 132–154.
  Translation: Goetze 1950: 399–400; Bernabé 1987: 263–266.
  Discussion: Neu 1983: 393–396.

6. Hurrian Prayer of Taduhepa to Tessub for the Well-being of Tasmi-sarri
   Text: CTH 777.8 (=ChS I/1, 41): KUB 32.19 + KBo 27.99 + KBo 15.73.
   Transliteration: Haas 1984: 215–232.
   Discussion: Kammenhuber 1976: 173; Wilhelm 1991: 40–47.

7. Prayer to the Sun-goddess of Arinna Concerning Plague and Enemies
   Text: CTH 376: C. KUB 24.4 + KUB 30.12. D. VBoT 121. G. KBo 7.63.
   Edition: Gurney 1940: 17–39; Güterbock 1958: 244; Carruba 1969: 239–242; Lebrun 1980: 159–164.
   Discussion: Carruba 1969: 237, 239ff., 247 n. 40; Houwink ten Cate 1970: 5, 68 f.; Neu/Rüster 1975: 3–5; Gurney 1977b: 200; Güterbock 1978: 136.

Mursili's Prayers Concerning Plague and Enemies

8. Mursili's Hymn and Prayer to the Sun-goddess of Arinna
   Text: CTH 376: A. KUB 24.3 + 544/u + KUB 31.144 + 401/u + 1947/u. B. KUB 30.13. [C and D = no. 7]. E. KUB 36.80. [F. = no. 16]. [G. = no. 7]. H. 79/w. I. 95/w. J. 1229/u (ZA 81: 110).
   Edition: Gurney 1940: 16–39 ("Copy C"); Lebrun 1980: 155–171; Güterbock 1980.
   Translation: Goetze 1955: 396; Bernabé 1987: 267–271; Ünal 1991: 803–808; Haas 1994: 431.
   Discussion: Güterbock 1958: 244; Carruba 1983.

9. Mursili's Hymn and Prayer to Telipinu
   Text: CTH 377: A. KUB 24.1 + 1122/v + 217/w (ZA 62: 232). B. KUB 24.2.
   Edition: Gurney 1940: 16–23; Lebrun 1980: 180–191.
   Translation: Goetze 1950: 396–397; Bernabé 1987: 273–275; Christmann-Franck 1989: 47–50.

10. Mursili's "Third" Plague Prayer to the Sun-goddess of Arinna
    Text: CTH 378. III: KUB 14.12.
    Edition: Goetze 1930: 236–241; Lebrun 1980: 216–219.

Translation: Furlani 1936: 267–275; Christmann-Franck 1989: 56–57; Beckman 1997a: 159.
Discussion: Furlani 1934.

11. Mursili's "Second" Plague Prayer to the Storm-god of Hatti
    Texts: CTH 378.II: A. KUB 14.8. B. KUB 14.11 + 650/u. C. KUB 14.10 + KUB 26.86.
    Edition: Goetze 1930: 204–235; 1955: 394–396; Lebrun 1980: 203–216.
    Translation: Furlani 1936: 267–275; Goetze 1950: 393–401; Kühne 1978: 169–174; Bernabé 1987: 279–284; Christmann-Franck 1989: 53–56; Beckman 1997a: 157–159.
    Discussion: Furlani 1934; Güterbock 1964: 112; 1978: 231; Archi 1978: 81–89.

12. Mursili's "First" Plague Prayer to the Assembly of Gods and Godesses.
    Texts: CTH 378.I: A. KUB 14.14 + KUB 19.1 + KUB 19.2 + KBo 3.47 + 1858/u + Bo 4229 + Bo 9433. B. KUB 23.3.
    Edition: Goetze 1930: 164–177; Lebrun 1980: 193–203.
    Translation: Furlani 1936: 267–275; Christmann-Franck 1989: 51–53; Ünal 1991: 808–811; Beckman 1997a: 156–157.
    Discussion: Furlani 1934.

13. Mursili's "Fourth" Plague Prayer to the Assembly of Gods (arranged by localities).
    Text: CTH 378.IV: A. KUB 14.13 + KUB 23.124. B. KBo 22.71.
    Edition: Goetze 1930: 242–251; Lebrun 1980: 220–239.
    Translation: Furlani 1936: 267–275; Beckman 1997a: 159–160.
    Discussion: Furlani 1934.

14. Mursili's "Fifth" Plague Prayer to the Assembly of Gods (arranged typologically)
    Text: CTH 379: KUB 48.111 + KUB 31.121 (+) KUB 31.121a.
    Edition: Güterbock 1960: 59–61; Lebrun 1980: 240–247; Sürenhagen 1985: 3–16.
    Discussion: Forrer 1926: 23–24; Houwink ten Cate 1987: 19–20; Singer 1996: 152–153.

Mursili's Prayers Concerning His Wife and His Stepmother

15. Mursili's Prayer to Lelwani for the Recovery of Gassuliyawiya
    Text: CTH 380: A. KBo 4.6. B. (?): 161/u. C. (?) 638/v. D. (?) 335/e.
    Edition: Lebrun 1980: 248–255; Tischler 1981.
    Translation: Ünal 1991: 811–813; de Roos 1983: 220–223.
    Discussion: Kümmel 1967: 120f.; Gurney 1977: 55; Otten 1984; Hoffner 1985; Dinçol et al. 1993: 98.

16. Mursili's Prayer to the Sun-goddess of Arinna for the Recovery of Gassuliyawiya
    Text: CTH 376. F: KUB 36.81.
    Edition: Lebrun 1980: 157, 166.
    Discussion: Güterbock 1958: 244; 1978: 137; Carruba 1983: 9f.

17. Mursili's Accusations Against Tawannanna
    Text: CTH 70: KUB 14.4.
    Edition: Cornelius 1975; de Martino 1998.
    Discussion: Forrer 1926: 1–3; Laroche 1956: 101–103; Bin-Nun 1975: 177–193; Van den Hout 1998: 42–44.

18. Mursili's Exculpation for the Deposition of Tawannanna
    Text: CTH 71: A. KBo 4.8 + "Izmir 1277." B. 1206/u + 245/w.
    Edition: Cornelius 1975; Hoffner 1983.
    Discussion: Laroche 1956: 101–103; Güterbock 1958: 244; Bin-Nun 1975: 189 ff.; Bryce 1998: 227–230.

Muwatalli's Prayers

19. Muwatalli's Prayer to the Storm-god Concerning the Cult of Kummanni
    Text: CTH 382: KBo 11.1.
    Edition: Houwink ten Cate/Josephson 1967; Lebrun 1980: 294–308.
    Translation: de Roos 1983: 224–228; Bernabé 1987: 293–297.
    Discussion: Singer 1996: 161–164.

20. Muwatalli's Model Prayer to the Assembly of Gods through the Storm-god of Lightning
    Text: CTH 381: A. KUB 6.45 + 1111/z + KUB 30.14. B. KUB 6.46. C. KUB 12.35. D. 1785/u.
    Edition: Lebrun 1980: 256–293; Singer 1996.

Translation: Goetze 1950: 397–399 (partial); Bernabé 1987: 285–292.
Discussion: Garstang/Gurney 1959: 116–119; Houwink ten Cate 1968; Haas 1998; Hutter 1998; Popko 1998.

Prayers of Hattusili, Puduhepa, and Tudhaliya

21. Hattusili's Prayer of Exculpation to the Sun-goddess of Arinna
   Text: CTH 383: KUB 21.19 + 1193/u (ZA 66: 104) (+) KUB 14.7+ 1303/u (+) Bo 4222 + 338/v (joinsketch in Marazzi 1983: 336).
   Edition: Lebrun 1980: 309–328; Sürenhagen 1981: 88–108; Singer 2002a (1193/u).
   Translation: de Roos 1983: 228–232.
   Discussion: Haas 1970; Archi 1971; Ünal 1973; Marazzi 1983: 331–340; Houwink ten Cate 1987: 21–22; Güterbock 1988; Singer 2001: 398 f.

22. Puduhepa's Prayer to the Sun-goddess of Arinna and Her Circle for the Well-being of Hattusili
   Text: CTH 384: KUB 21.27 + 676/v + 546/u + 695/v.
   Edition: Lebrun 1980: 329–347; Sürenhagen 1981: 108–122.
   Translation: Goetze 1950: 393–394; Bernabé 1987: 299–303; Ünal 1991: 813–817.
   Discussion: Archi 1971; Ünal 1973; Otten 1975: 20ff.; Marazzi 1983: 337–340; Fontaine 1987; Güterbock 1988; Parker 1998: 280; Singer 2001: 398 f.

23. Fragments of Prayers to the Storm-god of Nerik
   1st passage: *Evocatio*
   Text: CTH 386.1: KUB 36.90.
   Edition: Haas 1970: 175–183; Lebrun 1980: 363–365, 369–370.
   2nd passage: *Hymn*
   Text: CTH 386.2: KUB 31.136.
   Edition: Haas 1970: 196–199; Lebrun 1980: 366, 370.
   3rd passage: *Confession*
   Text: CTH 386.3: KUB 36.87.
   Edition: Haas 1970: 188–195; Lebrun 1980: 366–368, 371.

24. Tudhaliya's Prayer to the Sun-goddess of Arinna for Military Success
   Text: CTH 385.9: KBo 12.58 + KBo 13.162.
   Edition: Lebrun 1980: 357–361.
   Discussion: Houwink ten Cate 1986: 110; Catsanicos 1991: 23–24.

Concordance

CTH	Title of Prayer	Text
70	Mursili's Accusations Against Tawannanna	17
71	Mursili's Exculpation for the Deposition of Tawannanna	18
371	To the Sun-goddess of the Earth against Slander	1
372	A mortal to the Sun-god	4c
373	Kantuzzili to the Sun-god	4a
374	A king to the Sun-god	4b
375	Arnuwanda and Asmunikal to the Sun-goddess of Arinna	5
376.A	Mursili to the Sun-goddess of Arinna	8
376.C	To the Sun-goddess of Arinna Concerning Plague (Middle Hittite)	7
376.F	Mursili to the Sun-goddess for the Recovery of Gassuliyawiya	16
377	Mursili to Telipinu	9
378.I	Mursili's "First" Plague Prayer to the Assembly of Gods	12
378.II	Mursili's "Second" Plague Prayer to the Storm-god of Hatti	11
378.III	Mursili's "Third" Plague Prayer to the Sun-goddess of Arinna	10
378.IV	Mursili's "Fourth" Plague Prayer to the Assembly of Gods	13
379	Mursili's "Fifth" Plague Prayer to the Assembly of Gods	14

380	Mursili to Lelwani for the Recovery of Gassuliyawiya	15
381	Muwatalli to the Assembly of Gods	20
382	Muwatalli to the Storm-god Concerning Kummanni	19
383	Hattusili's Exculpation to the Sun-goddess of Arinna	21
384	Puduhepa to the Sun-goddess of Arinna and Her Circle	22
385.9	Tudhaliya to the Sun-goddess of Arinna for Military Success	24
385.10	To the Sun-goddess of Arinna for Protection of Royal Couple	3
386.1–3	Fragments of Prayers to the Storm-god of Nerik	23
389.2	To the Sun-god and the Storm-god against Slander	2
777.8	Taduhepa to Tesub for the Well-being of Tasmi-sarri (Hurrian)	6

Bibliography

Archi, A.
    1971   "The Propaganda of Ḫattušiliš III." *SMEA* 14: 185–215.
    1977   "I poteri della dea Ištar ḫurrita-ittita." *Oriens Antiquus* 16: 297–311.
    1978   "La peste presso gli ittiti." *Parola del Passato* 179: 81–89.
    1980   "Le testimonianze oracolari per la regina Tawannanna." *SMEA* 22: 19–29.
    1988   "Eine Anrufung der Sonnengöttin von Arinna." Pp. 5–31 in *Documentum Asiae Minoris Antiquae. Festschrift für Heinrich Otten zum 75. Geburtstag.* Ed. by E. Neu and Ch. Rüster. Wiesbaden: Harrassowitz.

Assmann, J.
    1991   "Ägyptische Hymnen und Gebete." Pp. 827–928 in *TUAT* Band II Lfg. 6 "Lieder und Gebete II." Gütersloher Verlagshaus Gerd Mohn.

Barucq, A., and F. Daumas
    1980   *Hymnes et prières de l'Egypte.* Paris: Cerf.

Beal, R.
    1986   "The History of Kizzuwatna and the Date of the Šunaššura Treaty." *Or* 55: 424–445.
    1992   *The Organisation of the Hittite Military (THeth 20).* Heidelberg: Carl Winter.

Beckman, G. M.
    1983a   *Hittite Birth Rituals* (StBoT 29). Wiesbaden: Harrassowitz.
    1983b   "Mesopotamians and Mesopotamian Learning at Hattuša." *JCS* 35: 97–114.
    1986   "Proverbs and Proverbial Allusions in Hittite." *JNES* 45: 19–30.

1990   Review of Hutter 1988, *BiOr* 47: 159–162.
1996   *Hittite Diplomatic Texts*. SBL Writings from the Ancient World Series, vol. 7. Atlanta: Scholars Press.
1997a   "Plague Prayers of Muršili II." Pp. 156–160 in *CoS I*.
1997b   "Proverbs" and "Other Wisdom Literature." Pp. 215–217 in *CoS I*.

Beckman, G. M., and H. A. Hoffner, Jr.
1985   "Hittite Fragments in American Collections." *JCS* 37/1.

Bernabé, A.
1987   *Textos literarios hetitas*. Madrid: Alianza Editorial.

Bin-Nun, Sh. R.
1975   *The Tawananna in the Hittite Kingdom (THeth 5)*. Heidelberg: Carl Winter.

Bryce, T.
1998   *The Kingdom of the Hittites*. Oxford: Clarendon Press.

Carruba, O.
1969   "Die Chronologie der Heth. Texte und die Heth. Geschichte der Grossreichszeit." *Zeitschrift der Deutschen Morgenländischen Gesellschaft*, Suppl. I: 226–249.
1983   "Saggio sulla preghiera etea (a proposito di CTH 376)." Pp. 3–27 in *Studi orientalistici in ricordo di Franco Pintore (StMed 4)*. O. Carruba, M. Liverani, C. Zaccagnini, eds. Pavia: GJES Edizioni.
1998   "Tawananna I. Babylonia Hieroglyphica." *ZA* 88: 14–126.

Catsanicos, J.
1991   *Recherches sur le Vocabulaire de la Faute. Apports du Hittite à l'étude de la phraséologie indo-européenne* (Cahiers de NABU 2). Paris: SEPOA.

Çeçen, S.
1995   "*mūtānū* in den Kültepe-Texten." Pp. 101–102 in *Atti del II Congresso Internazionale di Hittitologia*. O. Carruba, M. Giorgieri, C. Mora, eds. Pavia: Gianni Iuculano.

Christmann-Franck, L.
1989   "Hymnes et prières aux dieux Hittites." Pp. 40–57 in *Prières de l'Ancien Orient*. Paris: Cerf.

Cohen, M. E.
1988   *The Canonical Lamentations of Ancient Mesopotamia*. Potomac, MD: CDL.

Cohen, Y.
1997   "Taboos and Prohibitions in Hittite Society: A Study of the

Hittite Expression *natta āra* ('not right')." M.A. Thesis. Tel Aviv University.
2002 *Taboos and Prohibitions in Hittite Society: A Study of the Hittite Expression natta āra* ('not permitted') (*THeth 24*). Heidelberg: Carl Winter.

Collins, B.-J.
1997 (Hittite) "Rituals and Incantations." Pp. 160–177 in *CoS I*.

Cooper, J. S.
1972 "Bilinguals from Boghazköi II." *ZA* 62: 62–81.

Cornelius, F.
1975 "Ein hethitischer Hexenprozess." *Revue internationale des droits de l'antiquité* 22: 27–45.

Darga, M.
1974 "Puduhepa: An Anatolian Queen of the Thirteenth Century B.C." Pp. 939–961 in *Mélanges Mansel (Festschrift Arif Müfid Mansel)* 2. Ankara: Turk Tarih Kurumu Basimevi.

De Martino, S.
1991 "Himuili, Kantuzili e la presa del potere da parte di Tuthaliya." *Eothen* 4: 5–21.
1992 "Personaggi e riferimenti storici nel testo oracolare ittito KBo XVI 97." *SMEA* 29: 33–46.
1998 "Le accuse di Muršili II alla regina Tawananna secondo il testo KUB XIV 4." *Eothen* 9: 19–48.

Del Monte, G. F.
1993 *L'annalistica ittita*. Brescia: Paideia.

Dinçol, A. M., B. Dinçol, J. D. Hawkins, and G. Wilhelm
1993 "The 'Cruciform Seal' from Boğazköy/Hattusa." *Istanbuler Miteilungen* 43: 87–106.

Durand J.-M., and E. Laroche
1982 "Fragments hittites du Louvre." Pp. 73–107 in *Mémorial Atatürk: Études d'archéologie et de philologie anatoliennes*. Paris: Editions Recherche sur les civilisations.

Edzard, D. O.
1994 "Sumerische und akkadische Hymnen." Pp. 19–32 in *Hymnen der Alten Welt im Kulturvergleich*. W. Burkert, F. Stolz, eds. Freiburg Schweiz: Universitätsverlag.

Engelhard, D. H.
1970 "Hittite Magical Practices: An Analysis." Brandeis University Ph.D.diss. Ann Arbor: UMI.

Ertekin A, I. Ediz, and A. Ünal
　1993　"The Unique Sword from Boğazköy/Ḫattuša." Pp. 719–725 in *Studies in Honor of Nimet Özgüç*, M. Mellink, E. Porada, T. Özgüç, eds. Ankara: Türk Tarih Kurumu Basimevi.

Farber, W.
　1995　"Witchcraft, Magic, and Divination in Ancient Mesopotamia." Pp. 1895–1909 in *CANE III*.

Falkenstein, A., and W. von Soden
　1953　*Sumerische und Akkadische Hymnen und Gebete*. Zürich und Stuttgart: Artemis.

Fontaine, C. R.
　1987　"Queenly Proverb Performance: The Prayer of Puduḫepa (KUB XXI,27)." Pp. 95–126 in *The Listening Heart. Essays in Wisdom and the Psalms in Honor of Roland E. Murphy, O. Carm*. Ed. K. G. Hoglund, E. F. Huwiler, J. T. Glass, and R. W. Lee. Journal for the Study of the Old Testament, Supplement Series 5. Sheffield: Sheffield Academic Press.

Forrer, E.
　1926　Forschungen 2. Band. 1. Heft. Berlin: Privately published.

Foster, B. R.
　1993　*Before the Muses: An Anthology of Akkadian Literature*. Bethesda, MD: CDL.

Friedrich, J.
　1952　*Hethitisches Wörterbuch*. Heidelberg, Carl Winter Universitätsverlag.
　1954–55　"'Angst' und 'Schrecken' als niedere Gottheiten bei Griechen und Hethitern." *AfO* 17: 148.
　1957　"Ein hethitisches Gebet an die Sonnengöttin der Erde." *Rivista degli Studi Orientali* 32: 217–224.

Furlani, G.
　1934　"Muršiliš II e il concetto del peccato presso gli Hittiti." Pp. 19–37 in *Studi e Materiali di Storia delle Religioni*. Bologna: Nicola Zanichelli.
　1936　*La religione degli Hittiti* (Storia delle Religioni 13). Bologna: Nicola Zanichelli.

Furlani, G., and H. Otten
　1957–
　1971　"Gebet und Hymne in Hatti." *Reallexikon der Assyriologie* 3: 170–175.

Garstang, J., and O. R. Gurney
　1959　*The Geography of the Hittite Empire*. London: British Institute of Archaeology at Ankara.

Goetze, A.
- 1930 "Die Pestgebete des Muršiliš." Pp. 161–251 in *Kleinasiatische Forschungen* I/2. Weimar.
- 1933 *Die Annalen des Muršiliš.* Leipzig: J.C. Hinrichs'sche Buchhandlung.
- 1950 "Hittite Prayers." Pp. 120–128 in *Ancient Near Eastern Texts Relating to the Old Restament.* J. B. Pritchard, ed. Princeton. (repr. without changes in 1969).
- 1957 *Kulturgeschichte Kleinasiens.* Munich: C.H. Beck.

Görke, S.
- 2000 *Das Gebet des hethitischen Priesters Kantuzili.* M.A. thesis, Freie Universität Berlin.

Greenberg, M.
- 1994 "Hittite Royal Prayers and Biblical Petitionary Psalms." Pp. 15–27 in *Neue Wege der Psalmenforschung.* K. Seybold, E. Zenger, eds. Freiburg: Herder.

Gurney, O. R.
- 1940 "Hittite Prayers of Mursili II." *Annals of Archaeology and Anthropology* 27: 1–167.
- 1977a *Some Aspects of Hittite Religion.* Oxford University Press.
- 1977b Review of Neu — Rüster 1975. *OLZ* 34: 199–200.

Güterbock, H. G.
- 1958 "The Composition of Hittite Prayers to the Sun." *JAOS* 78: 237–245.
- 1960 "Mursili's accounts of Suppiluliuma's dealings with Egypt." *RHA* 66: 57–63.
- 1964 "A View of Hittite Literature." *JAOS* 84: 107–115.
- 1974 "Appendix (to Lambert 1974): Hittite Parallels." *JNES* 33: 323–327.
- 1978 "Some Aspects of Hittite Prayers." Pp. 125–139 in *The Frontiers of Human Language.* Ed. by T. R. Segerstedt. Uppsala: Acta Universitatis Upsaliensis.
- 1980 "An Addition to the Prayer of Muršili to the Sungoddess and its Implications." *Anatolian Sudies* 30: 41–50.
- 1984 "A Hurro-Hittite Hymn to Ishtar." Pp. 155–164 in *Studies in Literature from the Ancient Near East Dedicated to Samuel Noah Kramer* (American Oriental Series 65). J.M. Sasson, ed. New Haven.
- 1988 "Hethitisch *kurkurāi-* und Verwandtes." Pp. 115–119 in *Documentum Asiae Minoris Antiquae. Festschrift für Heinrich*

Otten zum 75. Geburtstag. E. Neu and Ch. Rüster, eds. Wiesbaden: Harrassowitz.

Haas, V.
1970 *Der Kult von Nerik* (Studia Pohl 4). Rome: Pontifical Institute.
1984 *Die Serien itkaḫi und itkalzi des AZU-Priesters, Rituale für Tašmišarri und Tatuḫepa sowie weitere Texte mit Bezug auf Tašmiššari*. Corpus der hurritischen Sprachddenkmäler, I/1. Rome: Multigrafica Editrice.
1985 "Betrachtungen zur Dynastie von Hattusa im Mittleren Reich (ca. 1450–1380)." *AoF* 12: 269–277.
1994 *Geschichte der hethitischen Religion*. Handbuch der Orientalistik. 1/15. Leiden: Brill.
1998 Review of Singer 1996. *Or* 67: 135–139.

Hallo, W. W.
1997 *The Context of Scripture*. Volume One: *Canonical Compositions from the Biblical World*. Leiden: Brill.

Hecker, K.
1989 "Akkadische Hymnen und Gebete." Pp. 718–783 in *TUAT* Band I. Lfg. 5. "Lieder und Gebete II." Gütersloher Verlagshaus Gerd Mohn.

Hoffner, H.A. Jr.
1973 "The Hittite Particle -*PAT*." Pp. 99–117 in *Festschrift Heinrich Otten*. Ed. E. Neu and Ch. Rüster. Wiesbaden: Harrassowitz.
1977 "Studies in Hittite Vocabulary, Syntax, and Style." *JCS* 29: 151–156.
1980 Review of J. Friedrich — A. Kammenhuber, *Hethitisches Wörterbuch*. Lieferungen 2–3. *BiOr* 37: 199–202.
1983 "A Prayer of Muršili II About His Stepmother." *JAOS* 103: 187–192.
1985 Review of Tischler 1981. *JNES* 44: 156–159.
1986 "Studies in Hittite Grammar." Pp. 83–94 in *Kaniššuwar. A Tribute to Hans G. Güterbock on his Seventy-Fifth Birthday*. Ed. H. A. Hoffner, Jr. and G.M. Beckman. Chicago: Oriental Institute.
1987 "Paskuwatti's Ritual Against Sexual Impotence (CTH 406)." *AuOr* 5: 271–287.
1990 *Hittite Myths*. Writings from the Ancient World 2. Atlanta: Scholars Press.
1997 *The Laws of the Hittites. A Critical Edition*. Leiden: Brill.

van den Hout, Th.
- 1995 "Khattushili III, King of the Hittites." Pp. 1107–1120 in *CANE II*.
- 1997 "Apology of Hattušili III." Pp. 199–204 in *CoS I*.
- 1998 *The Purity of Kingship. An Edition of CTH 569 and Related Hittite Oracle Inquiries of Tuthaliya IV*. Documenta et Monumenta Orientis Antiqui 25. Leiden: Brill.

Houwink ten Cate, Ph. H. J.
- 1968 "Muwatallis' 'Prayer to be Spoken in an Emergency,' an Essay in Textual Criticism." *JNES* 27: 204–208.
- 1969 "Hittite Royal Prayers." *Numen* 16: 81–98.
- 1970 *The Records of the Early Hittite Empire (c. 1450–1380 B.C.)*. Istanbul: Nederlands Historisch-Archaeologisch Instituut.
- 1974 "The Early and Late Phases of Urhi-Tesub's Career." Pp. 123–150 in *Anatolian Studies Presented to Hans Gustav Güterbock on the Occasion of his 65th Birthday*. Ed. K. Bittel, Ph. H. J. Houwink ten Cate, and E. Reiner. Istanbul: Nederlands Historisch-Archaeologisch Instituut in het Nabije Oosten.
- 1986 "Brief Comments on the Hittite Cult Calendar: The Outline of the AN.TAH.ŠUM Festival." Pp. 95–110 in *Kaniššuwar. A Tribute to Hans G. Güterbock on his Seventy-Fifth Birthday*. Ed. H. A. Hoffner, Jr. and G. M. Beckman. Chicago: Oriental Institute.
- 1987 "The Sun God of Heaven, the Assembly of Gods, and the Hittite King." Pp. 13–34 in *Effigies Dei. Essays on the History of Religions*. Ed. D. van der Plas. Leiden: Brill.
- 1994 "Urhi-Tesub revisited." *BiOr* 51: 233–259.
- 1996 "The Hittite Dynastic Marriages of the Period between ca. 1258 and 1244 B.C." *AoF* 23: 40–75.

Houwink ten Cate, Ph. H. J., and F. J. Josephson
- 1967 "Muwatallis' Prayer to the Storm-god of Kummanni (KBo XI 1)." *RHA* 25: 101–140.

Hutter, M.
- 1988 *Behexung, Entsühnung und Heilung. Das Ritual der Tunnawiya für ein Königspaar aus mittelhethitischer Zeit*. Orbis Biblicus et Orientalis 82. Freiburg: Universitätsverlag; Göttingen: Vandenhoeck & Ruprecht.
- 1991 "Bemerkungen zur Verwendung magischer Rituale in mittelhethitischer Zeit." *AoF* 18: 332–43.

1998 Review of Singer 1996. *BiOr* 55: 215–217.
Imparati, F.
1977 "Le istituzioni cultuali del ⁿᵃ⁴ḫekur e il potere centrale ittita." *SMEA* 18: 19–64.
1979 "Une reine de Hatti vénère la déesse Ningal." Pp. 169–176 in *Florilegium Anatolicum: Mélanges offerts à Emmanuel Laroche*. Paris.
Jacobsen, T.
1976 *The Treasures of Darkness: A History of Mesopotamian Religion*. New Haven: Yale University Press.
Jakob-Rost, L.
1997 *Keilschrifttexte aus Boghazköy im Vorderasiatischen Museum* (Vorderasiatische Schriftdenkmäler der Staatlichen Museen zu Berlin, Neue Folge, Heft XII). Mainz: Philipp von Zabern.
Kammenhuber, A.
1974 "Hethitische Gebete." Pp. 4412–4413 in *Kindlers Literatur Lexikon*, Band X.
1976 *Orakelpraxis, Träume und Vorzeichenschau bei den Hethitern* (THeth 7). Heidelberg: Carl Winter Universitätsverlag.
Kellerman, G.
1978 "The King and the Sun-god in the Old Hittite Period." *Tel Aviv* 5: 199–208.
1983 "Les prières hittites: A propos d'une récente monographie." *Numen* 30: 269–280.
Klengel, H.
1999a *Geschichte des hethitischen Reiches* (HbOr I/34). Leiden: Brill.
1999b "Epidemien im spätbronzezeitlichen Syrien-Palästina." Pp. 187–193 in *Michael. Historical, Epigraphical and Biblical Studies in Honor of Prof. Michael Heltzer*. Ed. Y. Avishur and R. Deutsch. Tel-Aviv-Jaffa: Archaeological Center Publications.
Klinger, J.
1996 *Untersuchungen zur Rekonstruktion der hattischen Kultschicht* (StBoT 37). Wiesbaden: Harrassowitz.
Klinger, J., and E. Neu
1990 "War die erste Computer-Analyse des Hethitischen verfehlt?" *Hethitica* 10: 135–160.
Košak, S.
1982 *Hittite Inventory Texts* (CTH 241–250) (THeth 10). Heidelberg: Carl Winter Universitätsverlag.

Bibliography

1998   *Konkordanz der Keilschrifttafeln* III/1 (StBoT 42). Wiesbaden: Harrassowitz.

Kühne, C.
1975   "Hethitische Texte, II. Gebete." Pp. 169–204 in *Religionsgeschichtliches Textbuch zum Alten Testament* I. W. Beyerlin, ed. Göttingen: Vandenhoeck & Ruprecht.
1978   "Hittite Texts." Pp. 146–184 in *Near Eastern Religious Texts Relating to the Old Testament.* W. Beyerlin, ed. Philadelphia: Westminster Press.

Kümmel, H. M.
1967   *Ersatzrituale für den hethitischen König* (StBoT 3). Wiesbaden: Harrassowitz.

Lambert, W. G.
1974   "Dingir.šà.dib.ba Incantations." *JNES* 33: 267–322.

Laroche, E.
1951–52   "Fragments hittites de Genève." *RA* 45: 131–138, 184–194; *RA* 46: 42–50, 214.
1956   "Documents hiéroglyphiques hittites provenant du palais d'Ugarit." Pp. 97–160 in C. F.-A, Schaeffer, *Ugaritica III.* Paris: Paul Geuthner.
1964   "La prière hittite: vocabulaire et typologie." *Annuaire de l'École pratique des Hautes Études,* Ve Section, *Sciences Religieuses* 72: 3–29.
1971   *Catalogue des Textes Hittites.* Paris: Klincksieck.
1974   "Les dénominations des dieux 'antiques' dans les textes hittites." Pp. 175–185 in *Anatolian Studies Presented to Hans Gustav Güterbock on the Occasion of his 65th Birthday.* Ed. K. Bittel, Ph. H. J. Houwink ten Cate, and E. Reiner. Istanbul: Nederlands Historisch-Archaeologisch Instituut in het Nabije Oosten.

Lebrun, R.
1980   *Hymnes et Prières Hittites.* Collana Homo Religiosus 4. Louvain-la-Neuve: Centre d'Histoire des Religions.

Marazzi, M.
1981   "Note in margine ad alcuni testi di preghiera ittiti." *Vicino Oriente* 4: 27–35.
1983   "Inni e preghiere ittite. A proposito di un libro recente." *Studi e materiali di Storia delle Religioni* 49: 321–341.
1994   "Ma gli Hittiti scrivevano veramente su "legno"?" Pp. 131–160 in *Miscellanea di studi linguistici in onore di Walter Belardi.* Rome.

Marazzi, M., and H. Nowicki
1978   "Vorarbeiten zu den hethitischen Gebeten." *Oriens Antiquus* 17: 257–278.

Masson, E.
1991   *Le combat pour l'immortalité. Héritage indo-européen dans la mythologie anatolienne.* Paris: Presses Universitaires de France.

Melchert, H. C.
1977   *Ablative and Instrumental in Hittite.* Doctoral Thesis, Harvard.
1998   "Hittite *arku-* 'Chant, Intone' vs. *arkuwā(i)-* 'Make a Plea.'" *JCS* 50: 45–51.

Neu, E.
1983   "Überlieferung und Datierung der Kaškäer-Verträge." Pp. 391–399 in *Beiträge zur Altertumskunde Kleinasiens. Festschrift für Kurt Bittel.* R. M. Boehmer and H. Hauptmann, eds. Mainz: von Zabern.

Neu, E., and Chr. Rüster
1975   *Hethitische Keilschrift-Paläographie II.* (StBoT 21) Wiesbaden: Harrassowitz.

Otten, H.
1950   "Die Gottheit Lelvani der Boğazköy-Texte." *JCS* 4: 119–136.
1958   *Hethitische Totenrituale.* Berlin: Akademie-Verlag.
1962   "Aitiologische Erzählung von der Überquerung des Taurus." *ZA* 55: 156–168.
1975   *Puduhepa, eine hethitische Königin in ihren Textzeugnissen.* Akademie der Wissenschaften und der Literatur, Abhandlungen der Geistes- und Sozialwissenschaftlichen Klasse, NR. 1. Mainz: Franz Steiner.
1984   Review of Tischler 1981. *Indogermanische Forschungen* 89: 298–301.
1991   "Bemerkungen zum Hethitischen Wörterbuch V." *ZA* 81: 108–119.
1995   *Die hethitischen Königssiegel der frühen Grossreichszeit.* Mainz: Akademie der Wissenschaften und der Literatur.
2000   "Ein Siegelabdruck Dutḫalijas I.(?)." *Archäologischer Anzeiger* 2000: 375–376.

Otten, H., and Chr. Rüster
1975   "Textanschlüsse und Duplikate von Boğazköy-Tafeln (31–40)." *ZA* 64: 241–249.

Otten, H., and V. Souček
 1969 *Ein althetitisches Ritual für das Königspaar* (StBoT 8). Wiesbaden: Harrassowitz.

Parker, V.
 1998 "Reflexions on the Career of Hattušiliš III until the Time of his Coup d'État." *AoF* 25: 269–290.

Pecchioli Daddi, F.
 2000 "Un nuovo rituale di Muršili II." *AoF* 27: 344–358.

Popko, M.
 1994 *Zippalanda. Ein Kultzentrum im hethitischen Kleinsaien* (THeth 21). Heidelberg: Universitätsverlag C. Winter.
 1995 *Religions of Asia Minor.* Warsaw: Academic Publications Dialog.
 1998 Review of Singer 1996. *OLZ* 93: 460–464.

Pringle, J.
 1983 "Hittite Birth Rituals." Pp. 128–141 in *Images of Women in Antiquity.* A. Cameron and A. Kuhrt, eds. London & Canberra: Croom Helm.

Puhvel, J.
 1984- *Hittite Etymological Dictionary.* Berlin and New York: Mouton de Gruyter.

Reiner, E., and H. G. Güterbock
 1967 "The Great Prayer to Ishtar and Its Two Versions from Boğazköy." *JCS* 21: 255–266.

Römer, W. H. Ph.
 1989 "Hymnen in sumerischer Sprache." Pp. 645–647 in *TUAT* Band II Lfg. 5 "Lieder und Gebete I." Gütersloher Verlagshaus Gerd Mohn.

de Roos, J.
 1983 'Drie hittitische gebeden." Pp. 220–232 in *Schrijvend Verleden: Documenten uit het oude Nabije Oosten vertaald en toegelicht.* K. R. Veenhof, ed. Leiden/Zutphen: Ex Oriente Lux—Terra.
 1995 "Hittite Prayers." Pp. 1997–2005 in *CANE III.*

Rüster, Chr.
 1972 *Hethitische Keilschrift-Paläographie* (StBoT 20). Wiesbaden: Harrassowitz.

Sasson, J. M. ed.
 1995 *Civilizations of the Ancient Near East.* Vol. I-IV. New York: Scribner.

von Schuler, E.
1965 *Die Kaškäer.* Berlin: Walter de Gruyter.

Seux, M.-J.
1976 *Hymnes et prières aux dieux de Babylonie et d'Assyrie.* Paris.

Singer, I.
1985 "The Battle of Niḫriya and the End of the Hittite Empire." *ZA* 75: 100–123.
1991 "The Title 'Great Princess' in the Hittite Empire." *Ugarit-Forschungen* 23: 328–338.
1994 "'The Thousand Gods of Hatti': The Limits of an Expanding Pantheon." Pp. 81–102 in *Concepts of the Other in Near Eastern Religions* (Israel Oriental Studies 14). I. Alon, I. Gruenwald, and I. Singer, eds. Leiden: Brill.
1995 "Some Thoughts on Translated and Original Hittite Literature." Pp. 123–128 in *Language and Culture in the Near East* (Israel Oriental Studies 15). S. Izre'el and R. Drory, eds. Leiden: Brill.
1996 *Muwatalli's Prayer to the Assembly of Gods Through the Storm-god of Lightning.* Atlanta: Scholars Press.
1998 "From Ḫattuša to Tarḫuntašša: Some Thoughts on Muwatalli's Reign." Pp. 536–541 in *Acts of the IIIrd International Congress of Hittitology.* S. Alp and A. Süel, eds. Ankara.
2001 "The Fate of Hattusa during the Period of Tarhuntassa's Supremacy." *Kulturgeschichten. Altorientalische Studien für Volkert Haas zum 65. Geburtstag.* Th. Richter, D. Prechel, J. Klinger, eds. Saarbrücken: Saarbrücker Druckerei.
2002a "Danuhepa and Kurunta." *Anatolia Antica. Scritti in ricordo di Fiorella Imparati.* S. De Martino and F. Pecchioli Daddi, eds. Firenze.
2002b "Kantuzili the Priest and the Birth of Hittite Personal Prayer." *Silva Anatolica. Anatolian Studies Presented to Maciej Popko on the Occasion of his 65th Birthday.* P. Taracha, ed. Warsaw.

Sommer, F., and A. Falkenstein
1938 *Die hethitisch-akkadische Bilingue des Ḫattušili I. (Labarna II.).* Bayerischen Akademie der Wissenschaften: Munich.

Starke, F.
1977 *Die Funktion der dimensionalen Kasus und Adverbien im Althethitischen* (StBoT 23). Harrassowitz: Wiesbaden.
1979 "Halmašuit im Anitta-Text und die hetitische Ideologie vom Königtum." *ZA* 64: 47–120.

1990	*Untersuchung zur Stammbildung des keilschrift-luwischen Nomens* (StBoT 31). Wiesbaden: Harrassowitz.

Sürenhagen, D.
1981	"Zwei Gebete Hattusilis und der Puduhepa." *AoF* 8: 83–168.
1985	*Paritätische Staatsverträge aus Hethitischer Sicht. Zu historischen Aussagen und literarischer Stellung des Textes* CTH 379 (StMed 5). Pavia: Gianni Iuculano.

Taracha, P.
1999	"Hethitologische Miszellen." *Archiv Orientální* 67: 671–681.

Tischler, J.
1977-	*Hethitisches Etymologisches Glossar.* Innsbruck: Innsbrucker Beiträge zur Sprachwissenschaft.
1981	*Das hethitische Gebet der Gassulijawija.* Innsbruck: Institut für Sprachwissenschaft der Universität Innsbruck.

Trémouille, M.-C.
1997	ᵈ*Hebat, Une divinité Syro-Anatolienne.* Eothen 7. Firenze: LoGisma.

Ünal, A.
1973	*Hattušili III.* (THeth 7). Heidelberg: Carl Winter Universitätsverlag.
1991	"Hethitische Hymnen und Gebete." Pp. 791–817 in *TUAT.* Band II. Lfg. 6. "Lieder und Gebete II." Gütersloher Verlagshaus Gerd Mohn.
1996	*The Hittite Ritual of Ḫantitaššu from the City of Ḫurma against Troublesome Years.* Ankara: Turkish Historical Society.

Wegner, I.
1981	*Gestalt und Kult der Ištar-Šawuška in Kleinasien* (Alter Orient und Altes Testament 36), Kevelaer/Neukirchen-Vluyn: Neukirchener Verlag.

Wilhelm, G.
1989	*The Hurrians.* Warminster: Aris & Phillips Ltd.
1991	"Zur hurritischen Gebetsliteratur." Pp. 37–47 in *Ernten, was man sät. Festschrift für Klaus Koch zu seinem 65. Geburtstag.* D. R. Daniels, U. Glessmer, M. Rösel, eds. Neukirchen: Neukirchener Verlag.
1994	"Hymnen der Hethiter." Pp. 59–77 in *Hymnen der Alten Welt im Kulturvergleich.* W. Bulkert and F. Stolz, eds. Freiburg Schweiz: Universitätsverlag.

Wilhelm, G., and J. Boese
: 1987 "Absolute Chronologie und die hethitische Geschichte des 15. und 14. Jahrhunderts v. Chr." Pp. 74–117 in *High, Middle or Low? Acts of an International Colloquium on Absolute Chronology*. P. Åstrom, ed. Gothenburg: Paul Åstrom förlag.

Indexes

1. Persons

Abraham, 50
Aki-Tessub, 7, 85
Amminnaya (f.), 77f.
Annella (f.), 74, 76
Arma-Tarhunta, 109
Arnuwanda I, 11ff., 16, 29, 40ff., 50
Arnuwanda II, 47, 56f., 70, 75
Asmunikal (f.), 11ff., 16, 29, 40ff., 50

Bentesina, 71

Danuhepa (f.), 10, 17, 97f.
Danuhepa's son(s), 97f.

Egyptian king, 67
Egyptian widow, 17, 66, 68

Gassul(iy)awiya (f.), 4, 14, 16f., 18, 70ff.

Hantitassu, 24
Hattusili I, 22
Hattusili III, 3, 8ff., 11, 14, 17, 44, 70f., 77, 96ff., 101ff., 106, 109f.

Kantuzzili, 6, 8, 13f., 15, 17f., 30ff., 45

Lupakki, 17, 66f.
Lurma(-ziti), 7, 85

Mezzulla (f.), 74, 76
Mursili I, 16, 49

Mursili II, 5ff., 10f., 14, 16ff., 30, 40, 45f., 47ff., 70ff., 82, 86, 97
Mursili III, *see* Urhi-Tessub
Muwatalli I, 45
Muwatalli II, 6ff., 10, 12, 14f., 18, 50, 80ff., 96ff., 102

Nikalmati (f.), 30

Puduhepa (f.), 6, 8f., 11, 14f., 17, 44, 71, 96, 101ff., 109f.

Sharre-Kushuh, 74
Suppiluliuma I, 10, 14, 16, 29, 44, 47f., 56ff., 61f., 65, 70, 75, 82, 108
Suppiluliuma II, 14

Taduhepa (f.), 6, 9, 13, 29, 43f.
Tarhunta-zalma, 17, 66f.
Tasmi-Sarri, *see* Tudhaliya II
Tawannanna the Babylonian (f.), 10, 16f., 70ff., 97f.
Tudhaliya I, 18, 29f., 33, 45
Tudhaliya II/Tasmi-Sarri, 29, 43f., 47, 61, 65
Tudhaliya IV, 11, 14, 96f., 101, 106, 108ff.
Tudhaliya the Younger, 10, 16, 48, 61f.

Urhi-Tessub, 3, 10, 96ff., 102f., 110

Zuwa[-, 45f.

133

2. Deities

Ala, 89
Allani, 22
Allatum, 22, 71, 88
Ammama of Hanhana, 90
Annari, *see* Strength-deity
Anunnaki, *see* Netherworld gods
Angry god, 8, 30ff., 45, 103
Apara of Samuha, 88
Asgasipa, 88
assembly, gods of, 67
Aya, 88

Bunene, 31, 34, 37, 50

Calf, Prominent, 88

Damkina, 88
damnassara-deities, 59
Darawa, 22f.

Enlil, 31, 34, 36, 50
Ereshkigal, 22, 71, 106
Erra, 64
Estan, 22

Fate-goddesses, 67, 103, 110
"the Four," *see* quadriga
Fears (*nahsariattes*), 31, 34, 37

God, 50
god of Parsa, 89
gods of Hatti, 86ff., 93, 101
gods of His Majesty's father, 90
gods of His Majesty's grandfather, 90
gods of His Majesty's grandmother, 90
gods of the House of Gazzimara, 90
gods of the lands, 86ff., 94ff.

Halki, 67
Halmasuit, 88
Hantidassu of Hurma, 88
Hapandaliya, 88
Harnessing-god (Turesgala), 37
Hasammeli, 67

Hasigasnawanza of Lawazantiya, 88
Hatahha of Ankuwa, 90
Heaven and Earth, 82
Hebat, 15, 30, 81f., 86ff., 93, 101f.
Hebat of Apzisna, 90
Hebat of Halab, 88
Hebat of Halab of Hatti, 88
Hebat of Halab of Hurma, 88
Hebat of Kummanni, 67, 74, 76, 81, 88, 96
Hebat of Samuha, 87
Hebat of the *sinapsi*, 88
Hebat of Wasuduwanda, 90
Hebats, all, 67
Hebat-Sarruma(s), 67, 89
Hilassi, 22f.
Hulla, 67, 87
Hurri, 67, 87, 93
Hutanni, 81f.
Huwassana (GAZ.BA.IA) of Hupisna, 89
Huzzi, 81f.

Ishara of Astata, 74, 76
Ishtar/Sausga, 3, 67
Ishtar-*li*, 88
Ishtar of Haddarina, 88
Ishtar of Innuwita, 90
Ishtar of Nineveh, 88
Ishtar of Samuha, 67, 97
Ishtar of Sulama, 90
Ishtar of Wasuduwanda, 90
Ishtar of the Field, 90
Ishtar of the Field of His Majesty, 67
Ishtar of the Field of Samuha, 88
Ishtars, all, 67
Istanu, 30f., 49f.
Iyarri, 64, 67

Kamrusepa of Taniwanda, 64
Karmahi of Kalimuna, 90
Karuna of Kariuna, 90
Karzi, 88
Katahha, 90
King of gods, 81f.

King(ly) god of Hurniya, 89
Kubaba, 88

Lady of the *ayakku,* 88
LAMMA, *see* Protective-god
Lelwani/Liliwani, 9, 11, 67, 71ff., 101, 103f.
Lord of Lanta, 90
lulahi-gods, 88
Lusiti of Nenassa, 89

Marduk, 67
Mezzulla, 9, 11, 67, 81, 87, 101, 104f.
Mighty Goddess of Sahhaniya, 89
Misharu, 31, 34, 37, 50
Mother-goddesses, 67, 103, 110
Mulliyara, 88

nahsariattes, see Fears
Nawatiyala of Zarwisa, 89
Netherworld gods (Anunnaki), 8, 11, 15, 22, 37, 81, 83f., 103
Ningal, 31, 33, 36, 38, 50, 88

Paraya, 22f.
personal god, 8, 46, 50, 54, 86
Pirwa, 67, 88
Pirwa of Duruwaduruwa, 90
Pirwa of Iksuna, 90
Pirwa of Nenisakuwa, 90
Pisanuhi, 88
primeval gods, 34, 36f., 51, 61
Protective-god, 33, 35, 39, 46
Protective-god of Hatenzuwa, 88
Protective-god of Hatti, 67, 88
Protective-god of Kalasmitta, 90
Protective-god of Karahna, 89
Protective-god of the Army Camp of His Majesty's father in Marassantiya, 64
Protective-god of the Field, 90
Protective-god of the King, 90
Protective-god of the *kursas,* 88
Protective-god of the Sun-goddess of the Netherworld, 22f.
Protective-gods, all, 66f.

Queen of Paliya, 90

Sahhassara of Tuwanuwa, 89
Sarruma, 81f., 84, 97
Sarrumas, all, 67
Sausga, *see* Ishtar
Seri (the bull of the Storm-god), 9, 67, 81, 86, 87, 93
Servants of the Sun-goddess of the Netherworld, 22f.
Shamash, 3, 14, 31, 49
Sin, 31, 33, 38, 50
Storm-god, 7ff., 13, 17, 24f., 59, 67, 81f., 86, 93, 101, 104f., 107
Storm-god of Alazhana, 90
Storm-god of Apzisna, 90
Storm-god of Arinna, 87
Storm-god of Ar[ziya?], 64
Storm-god of Halab, 88
Storm-god of Halab of Hatti, 88
Storm-god of Halab of Hurma, 88
Storm-god of Harziuna, 89
Storm-god of Hasuna, 64
Storm-god of Hatra, 90
Storm-god of Hatti, 3, 8, 11, 49, 57ff., 67, 86, 88, 93, 96, 100
Storm-god of Hissashapa, 89
Storm-god of Hurma, 88
Storm-god of Hurniya, 89
Storm-god of Illaya, 89
Storm-god of Karahna, 89
Storm-god of Kuliwisna, 89
Storm-god of Kummanni, 81, 88
Storm-god of Lihzina, 64
Storm-god of Lightning (*pihassassi*), 9, 17, 81, 85ff., 91f., 96
Storm-god of Lihsina, 89
Storm-god of Mount Manuziya, 88
Storm-god of Nenassa, 89
Storm-god of Nerik(ka), 8f., 11, 40, 43, 81, 88, 97, 99, 101ff., 105ff.
Storm-god of Pahtima, 89
Storm-god of Parashunta, 90
Storm-god of [Pittiy]arik, 89
Storm-god of Sahhaniya, 89
Storm-god of Sahpina, 88
Stormgod of Sahhuwiya, 89

Storm-god of Sallapa, 90
Storm-god of Sarrisa, 88
Storm-god of Sugazziya, 89
Storm-god of Tegarama, 90
Storm-god of Tupazziya, 90
Storm-god of Tuwanuwa, 89
Storm-god of Uda, 89
Storm-god of Ussa, 90
Storm-god of Zarwisa
Storm-god of Zip(pa)landa, 9, 11, 67, 81, 86, 88, 93, 97, 101, 105
Storm-god *hulassassis*, 91
Storm-god *piha(i)mi* of Sanahuita, 67, 88
Storm-god of the *sinapsi*, 88
Storm-god of the Army, 88
Storm-god of the Growth, 90
Storm-god of the House of the *tawannanna*, 91
Storm-god of Life, 87
Storm-god, Noble (*multarihu*), 64, 69
Storm-god of the Rain, 90
Storm-god of the Ruin, 87, 89
Storm-god of Salvation, 87
Storm-god of Thunder, 88
Storm-god, Valiant (*muwatalli*), 69, 88
Storm-gods, all, 66f., 88
Storm-godly fashion, 92
Strength-deity (Annari), 35
Sun-god (of Heaven), 8f., 13, 15, 17, 24f., 30ff., 49, 67, 78, 81f., 86f., 91f.
Sun-god of Hatti, 88
Sun-god, Witness, 94
Sun-god(dess) of Malitaskuriya, 89
Sun-god(dess) of Washaniya, 90
Sun-goddess of Arinna, 3, 6ff., 11f., 15, 25ff., 40ff., 44f., 49ff., 56, 67, 73, 77, 81, 86ff., 91, 96ff., 101ff.
Sun-goddess of the Netherworld, 8f., 15, 21ff., 27, 67, 89
Suwanzipa of Suwanzana, 89

Tamisiya of Tapiqqa, 91
Tasimi, 89
Tazzuwasi, 88
Telipinu, 7, 9, 13, 49f., 53ff., 67, 88
Telipinu of Durmitta, 89
Telipinu of Hanhana, 90
Telipinu of Tawiniya, 90
Telipinus, all, 64
Terrors (*weritemas*), 31, 34, 37
Tessub, 9, 30, 43f.
Turesgala, *see* Harnessing-god
Two lords of Landa, 64

Uliliyassi of Parmanna, 64

Vizier of the Sun-goddess of the Netherworld, 22f.

War-god (ZABABA), 67, 88
War-god of Arziya, 88
War-god of Hupisna, 89
War-god of Illaya, 89
War-god of Nerik, 88
War-gods, all, 67
Washaliya of Harziuna, 89
weritemas, see Terrors

ZABABA, *see* War-god
Zahapuna, 88, 106
Zanduza of Sallapa, 90
Zintuhi, 9, 11, 67, 87, 101, 104
Zithariya, 88
Zulima, 89

3. Places

Alasiya, 16, 62
Alazhana, 90
Aleppo, 16, 49, 53
Amqa, 17, 47f., 58
Amurru, 71
Ankuwa, 64, 90
Apzisna, 90
Arawanna, 49, 52
Arinna, 11, 13, 26f., 45, 54, 64, 100f., 108

Places

Arusna, 85
Arzawa, 33, 36, 49, 52, 68, 106
Arziya, 64, 89
Ashtata, 74, 76, 79
Assuwa, 18
Assyrians, 108
Azzi/Hayasa, 75, 77

Babylon, 16, 49, 53, 74

Cedar Land, 15, 102
Comana Cappadociae, see Kummanni

Daha, Mount, 88
Dahalmuna, Mount, 106
Dankusna, 42
Durmitta, 64, 89
Duruwaduruwa, 90

Egypt(ians), 9f., 17, 47f., 57ff., 64ff., 80, 96, 110

Gazzimara, 90

Haharwa/Hahruwa, Mount, 88, 106
Hakm/pis, 40, 43, 90, 102, 106f.
Ha(n)hana, 64, 90, 108
Harpisa, (Mount), 90, 106
Harziuna, 89
Hasuna, 64
Hatra, 90
Hatti, 11, 15, 26, 29, 40ff., 48, 51ff., 64, 73ff., 88, 97ff., 102f., 107, 109
Hattina, 90
Hattusa, 8, 12f., 26, 29, 31, 40, 45, 54, 79f., 99ff., 102, 109
Hayasa, see Azzi
Himuwa, 42
Hulaya, River, 90
Hum[-, 43
Hupisna, 64, 89
Hurma, 64, 88
Hurna, 42
Hurniya, 89
Hurri(an) Land, 44, 68, 107
Hursama, 42

Huwalanuwanda, Mount, 90

Idalhamuna, Mount, 106
Iksuna, 90
Ilaluha, 42
Illaya, 64, 89
Innuwita, 90
Isuwa, 90

Jerusalem, 40

Kalasma, 49, 53
Kalasmitta, 90
Kalimuna, 90
Kallistapa, Mount, 88
Kammamma, 42
Kapiruha, 42
Karahna, 64, 89
Kariuna, 90
Karkamish, 74, 76, 79
Kaska(-land/-men), 11, 16, 29, 40ff., 49, 52, 80, 94, 102
Kastama, 42, 88
Katapa, 88, 99, 102
Kattila, 64
Kazzapa, 42
Kizzuwatna, 14, 29f., 44, 46, 50, 68, 76, 80ff., 95, 101
Kummanni, 7f., 67, 74, 76, 80ff., 88, 94, 107
Kurustamma, 17, 48, 58
Kuwapita, Mount, 110

Lanta, 90
Lawazantiya, 88
Lihs/zina, (Mount), 64, 89, 106
Lower Land, 90, 106
Lukka, 49, 53

Mala (Euphrates) River, 10, 48, 57ff.
Malitaskuriya, 89
Manuziya, 88
Marassantiya, 64
Marassantiya, River, 89, 106
Mittanni, 49, 52, 70
Muwani, 64

Nenassa, 89
Nenisakuwa, 90
Nerik(ka), 16f., 40, 42f., 88, 96f., 99, 101ff., 105ff., 109
Nerik, source of, 106

Pahtima, 89
Paliya, 90
Parashunta, 90
Parmanna, 64
Parsa, 89
Pataliya, 42
Pi/uskurunuwa, Mount, 88, 106
Pitassa, 49, 53
Puputana, 105

Qadesh, 80

Sahhaniya, 89
Sahhuwiya, 89
Sal(la)pa, 64, 90
Samuha, 64, 72, 87f.
Sarlaimi, Mount, 89
Sanahuita, 88
Sarissa, 64, 88
Serisa, 42
Shanhara (Babylon), 75, 79
Sipidduwa, 42
Sodom, 50
Sugazziya, 89
Sulama, 90
Summiyara, Mount, 88
Suwanzana, 89

Taggasta, 42
Tahali, Mount, 106
Tahatariya, 43

Takkupsa, 42, 88
Takurga, Mount, 90, 106, 108f.
Taniwanda, 64
Tapasawa, 42
Tapiqqa, 91
Tarhuntassa, 17, 80, 97f.
Tarugga, 42
Tastaressa, 42
Tatta, Mount, 88
Tawiniya, 90
Tegarama, 90
Tiwa, 87
Tuhasuna, 43
Tupazziya, 90
Tuwanuwa, 64, 89

Uda, 89
Ugarit, 70
Upper Land, 106
Ur, 40
Urauna, 88
Ussa, 90

Washaya, 42
Washaniya, 90
Wasuduwanda, 90

Zaliyanu, Mount, 88, 106
Zalpa, 106
Zalpuwa, 42
Zar(ru)wisa, 64, 89
Zazzisa, 64
Zihhana, 42
Zip(pa)landa, 13, 45, 64, 88, 101
Zithara, 88

[. . .]hulla, Mount, 106

4. Subjects

agony, 17, 31, 35, 39, 57, 71, 77
animals, 9, 34, 37, 91
anointing, 106
arawanna-ritual, 85
arkuwar (prayer), 5
assembly of gods, 5, 8f., 30, 61, 64ff., 67, 91, 100f., 103

atonement, *see* expiation
augurs, *see* oracular inquiries

Babylonian hymns and prayers, 3, 7, 14, 18, 31, 49
banishment from the palace, 70ff.
Biblical parallels, 2, 40

Subjects

bird, 17, 60, 92
birth(stool), 11, 32, 101, 103, 105
black magic, *see* sorcery
blind, 44
boat, 35, 39, 45
boundaries/borderlands, 36, 51, 58, 62, 67, 96
break an oath, 16, 32, 38, 40, 43, 48, 52, 57f., 62
breast, 17, 85
burnt offerings, 12, 86, 94

chief of the cleaners/barbers, 22f.
chief of the dignitaries/eunuchs, 22f.
child, 56, 67, 98
clouds, 91
collective punishment, 18, 48, 50, 53, 82, 84
colophons, 6, 97
confession, 16, 24, 81, 86
congregation, 12, 53, 56
corners of the land, 34, 36f.
cult calendar, 40ff., 51ff., 103, 108
cult inventory, 40ff., 51ff.
cult personnel, 40ff., 53ff.

dahanga, 100, 109
dark earth, *see* netherworld
deaf, 44
dead person, 84
death/dying, 7, 10, 17f., 31f., 38, 47, 56ff., 65, 74f., 77f., 100, 102
defamation, *see* slander
dictation, 14, 85
divination, *see* oracular inquiries
divine court, *see* assembly of gods
divine images, 41ff.
divine nature, 15
divine vengeance, 52, 62f., 84
divine weapon, 53, 55, 100, 102, 107
divine wrath, 10, 15f., 18, 47, 71, 81f.
diviner, *see* oracular inquiries
dream, *see* oracular inquiries
do ut des, 11
dog, 9, 34, 37, 91
door of heaven, *see* gate of heaven
dreams, *see* oracular inquiries

drought, 82
dumb, 44

east and west, 106
east, west, north, south, 107
effigy, 11, 101, 104
Egyptian prayers, 7, 18
endowment, 11, 102, 105
enemy (land), 6, 14, 16, 26, 29, 33, 44, 47ff., 50, 53f., 63, 100, 102, 108
evil bird, 84, 95
evil person, 9, 34, 37, 50, 53
evil tongue/word, *see* defamation
exculpation, 3, 10, 16, 71, 74f., 77, 82, 96ff.
expiation, 48ff., 81ff., 105, 109
eyelashes, 15, 22

famine, 55f.
festivals, *see* cult calendar

gate/door of heaven, 15, 34, 36, 51
gestures, 13
governors, 40, 43
Great Daughter, 71f.

Hattian rituals, 13
heaven and earth, 32, 34ff., 37, 51, 81f., 87, 91, 97, 103, 106
hekur-house of the Protective-god, 75
historical information, 16
house, *see* also palace
House of Gazzimara, 90
House of the *tawannanna*, 91
human condition, 18, 32, 38, 100
Hurrian influence, 14, 21, 29, 81
Hurrian hymns and prayers, 3f., 6, 9, 14, 29f., 43f.
Hurro-Luwian influence, 80
hymns, 2f., 5, 18

innocence, *see* exculpation
interceding, 8f., 22, 86, 91f., 101ff.
invocations, 4f., 13, 21ff., 54, 68, 76, 86
iron (peg), 24f., 107

just/good person, 36, 50, 53, 63

king's gate, 33, 39
kingship (ideology of), 21, 24f., 87, 91, 97, 99, 102
kursas, Protective-god of, 88

labarna, 25ff., 107
lapis lazuli, 36, 38, 50, 107
law and custom, 33, 36
legal suit, *see* trial procedure
lightning, 91
lion, 49, 53
literary tradition, 4
locusts, 55f.
Luwian rituals, 13
Luwian word, 95

man of god, *see* oracular inquiries
mankind, 52, 56, 65
mantalli ritual, 3
marianni-, 44
mazumazuwanta, 106
merchant, 17, 33, 35, 39
metaphors, 17, 24, 27, 35, 39, 103
Mesopotamian influence, 21, 25, 29f., 44
Mesopotamian lamentations, 40
Middle Hittite script or language, 21f., 24, 27, 30f., 33, 40, 44, 47f.
model prayer, 85f.
moonlight, 92
mortal/son of mankind, 6, 30, 34ff.
mother-of-god priestess, 77ff.
mountains, 16, 50, 54, 61, 82ff., 87ff., 94f., 106
mugawar (invocation), 5

neglect of cults, 10, 48, 57ff., 82, 107f.
netherworld/dark earth, 78, 85, 91, 107
new moon, 24f.
"not right" (*natta ara*), 10, 74, 98f., 109

offerings, 40ff., 86, 92ff., 103

offering ritual, 3, 12f., 22, 25 ff., 41, 86, 92ff.
offering tables, 12, 86, 92ff.
old age, 56f.
Old Assyrian period, 47
Old Hittite features, 21f., 24, 25, 30
old men, 82ff.
old women, *see* oracular inquiries
omen, *see* sun omen
oppressed person, 9, 34, 37, 53
oracular inquiries, 3f., 10, 16, 31, 35, 38f., 47, 52, 58ff., 63ff., 70f., 73, 77, 82, 84, 107
ornament, 104
orphans, 84
"orphan king," 11, 24, 33ff., 39, 91

palace of His Majesty, 89
palace of the grandfather, 87
perjury, *see* slander
personal prayers, 13f., 21, 29
pig, 9, 34, 37, 56, 91
plague, 7, 14, 17, 44, 47ff.
poor man, 84
postscript, 85, 94
priest of the Sun-goddess of Arinna, 7, 26f., 91
priestess, *see* mother-of-god
primordial order, 82
princes, 54ff., 92, 102
proofreading, 85
prostitution, 74
purification, 13, 62, 66, 103

queen(ship), 54ff., 92, 97
quadriga ("the Four"), 15, 31, 34, 37

rain, 56
religious reform, 80, 96, 101
restitution, *see* expiation
rituals, *see* offering ritual
rivers, 39, 45, 61, 82ff., 87ff., 94
roof, 12, 25, 27, 86

sacrosanct food, *see* taboos
salimani-, 12, 25f.
sarpa-, 52, 60, 68

scribe, 3, 7, 13, 49, 54, 65f.
sea, 15f., 35, 50, 54, 91, 106
seal, 25, 43
seer(ess), *see* oracular inquiries
seven times, 36, 45
shield, 11, 102, 105
sickness, 7ff., 17f., 31ff., 35, 38f., 70ff., 101ff.
sinapsi-sanctuary, 84, 88, 95
sins, 10, 24, 35, 38f., 47, 52, 59, 82, 86, 100, 108
slander, 13, 21ff., 74ff., 84, 99f., 103
snake, 17, 24f.
solar eclipse, 17, 75
sorcery, 16, 74
spear, 26
statue, *see* effigy
Stone House of the gods, 74f.
substitution rituals, 3, 16, 55, 71f.
suffering, *see* agony
sun, 17, 27f., 33, 35, 71, 82, 86
sun omen, 75ff.
swineherds, 49, 52
syncretism, 15

tabarna, 86

taboos, 16, 31ff., 38
tawannanna-, 25ff., 91, 107
temples, 11f., 15, 25, 27, 40ff., 50ff., 59, 63ff., 73, 91f., 108
transfer of gods, 98
throne, 44, 91
throne of the Storm-god, 84
thunder, 91
treaties, 9, 49
trial procedure, 3, 17, 96ff.

underground watercourses, 61

vows, 5, 11, 58, 101ff.

water, 85
weavers, 49, 52
wetnurse, 11, 100
wheels, 17, 24f.
winds, 91
wisdom literature, 17
wooden tablets, 95
words, unworthy, 85, 87
written records, 82, 84

Writings from the Ancient World

Edward F. Wente, *Letters from Ancient Egypt*, 1990.

Harry A. Hoffner, Jr., *Hittite Myths*, 1991; second edition, 1998.

Piotr Michalowski, *Letters from Early Mesopotamia*, 1993.

James M. Lindenberger, *Ancient Aramaic and Hebrew Letters*, 1994.

Martha T. Roth, *Law Collections from Mesopotamia and Asia Minor*, 1995; second edition, 1997.

William J. Murnane, *Texts from the Amarna Period in Egypt*, 1995.

Gary M. Beckman, *Hittite Diplomatic Texts*, 1996.

John L. Foster, *Hymns, Prayers, and Songs: An Anthology of Ancient Egyptian Lyric Poetry*, 1996.

Simon Parker et al., *Ugaritic Narrative Poetry*, 1997.

Dennis Pardee, *Ritual and Cult at Ugarit*, 2002.

Itamar Singer, *Hittite Prayers*, 2002.